THE BEAUTY
of FLIGHT

By Edward Clack

Copyright© 1993 by the author
First published in 1993
All rights reserved

ISBN 0-9520073-2-0

DEDICATION

To My Dear Wife

Cathy

who has waited many hours for me to come up
from beneath the waves,
and even more for me to come down
from above the clouds.

An Alpine Glacier

Front cover:
Margate, Kent · Mountfitchet Castle, Essex · Bassenthwaite Lake, Lake District
Bamburgh Castle, Northumberland · The River Thames from Waterloo Bridge

Why Are You So Beautiful?

(I asked the mountain)

"Why are you so beautiful?"
I asked the mountain

But the swirling mist descended
No more could I see the mountain

And waiting, saw the mist
lift, drift away to
Somewhere else
To cling to fonds of bracken
on sheep clad hills

"Why are you so beautiful?"
I asked the mountain

Aloof, the mountain
remained silent
I turned and walked away

"in the swirling mists
of time, I began..."
said a whisper...
from somewhere...

And the mist had bejewelled
the fleece
on the sheep
as I walked
on and on...
and away from a magic moment.

Aileen Otley.

Langdale Pikes

Contents

Published by

AIRBORNE ART

Air and ground photography by Edward Clack

The author wishes to thank the following:

Bird photography by Gerry Downy
Paintings by Ronald Slade
Reconstructing the past–Paintings by Peter Froste
Poems by Aileen Otley
From 'How The Lake District Was Made'
and 'Lake District Yellow Bonnets'

and
because I am unable to fly and take photographs at the same time, the following pilots:
Peter Ford; 'Hughes 500' helicopter above London
Alan Ward; various aircraft and sites
Derek Bidwell: various aircraft and sites
Peter Bell: Citabria, The Heritage Coast
Christopher Osborne: Piper Tomahawk around Kent
Bill Dixon: Cessna, Above The Lakes
Garry Giles: Cessna, Cock and Bull Story
Nino: Cessna, in the mountains of Italy

and to all the other pilots and other people who have added to his knowledge and experience
and made this book possible

Said my mother,
"What is all this story about?"
"A Cock and a Bull,"
said Yorick.
Laurence Sterne (1713-1768)

Stony Stratford and The Cock and The Bull

The Romans spread their influence through most of the known world centred on the Mediterranean, landing in the British isles near Dover in 55BC. A lighthouse used by the Romans is still standing in the bailey of Dover Castle. To maintain such a vast empire fast communications were required, so their engineers constructed a vast network of roads fanning out from Rome following gentle undulations of the countryside in straight lines, only deviating when the gradient would have been too steep.

From Dubrae (Dover) the roads again reached to encompass Britain, crossing the Thames at the first practical point at Londinium (London). From there they radiated in all directions, giving the legions rapid access to their forts, towns, and garrisons.

Now when flying above the countryside, the distinctive straight roads are a sure sign of their Roman origins. From Dubrae, Watling Street crossed Kent to Londinium; in London now the exact route is not clear. The road crossed the Thames somewhere near where London Bridge now stands. It is suggested that Park Lane is part of the line and from Marble Arch the Edgeware Road is once again 'Watling Street', a name which the road carries for much of the way through Verulanium (St. Albans) north west to Monmouth and beyond.

During pipe laying excavations in the Edgeware Road a section of the original Roman Watling Street was uncovered. It was a very solid construction: first there was 12 inches of rammed gravel with a layer of nodular flints set in lime grouting carefully laid on top. There was a kerb wall of gravel concrete to keep the edges in place. A superb piece of road building on this very important highway.

The construction and the network of roads was so good that the Roman road system was the main network of roads in this country until very recent times when bypasses were built round the towns which grew up on these 2000 year old roads, and motorways constructed.

I was flying with a student flying instructor Garry Giles near Milton Keynes,
"You see that straight road passing through the centre of that town? It is surely Roman in origin, probably Watling Street." I observed.

"That is interesting," he replied, and added, "The town is Stony Stratford and if you look down close by the church, in the centre are the inns, The Cock and The Bull. That is where the saying 'a Cock and Bull story' originated. So it was in the heyday of the stagecoach that these same routes were used and just as in Roman times, staging posts were established where the travellers could rest, take refreshment and tell tales.

Stony Stratford, sitting astride Watling Street, was one. There were twenty-four inns where horses could be changed, wenches wooed, thirst slaked with ale. Opposite the parish church under the sign of the Cock, was the great entrance to the stables. The stagecoach drivers and their passengers must have been pleased as the coach clattered to a halt in the stable yard. Horses were untethered, the driver and the travellers made their way into the inn warmed by a great log fire. After a few hours of revelry and story telling they would all go on a wobbly 'pub-crawl' a few yards along Watling Street to the Bull Inn. The eating, drinking and wenching would start again, but by now, under the influence of ale, and the company the tales had become embroidered.

So today, as a result of those early travellers, when stories seem to be exaggerated, we call them "Cock and Bull Stories."

While I was writing this my daughter Rosemary rang.

"Happy birthday Dad," she said, "what are you doing?"

"I'm writing a cock and bull story," I replied.

"What about?" she asked.

"A Cock and Bull," I said.

Dover Roman Lighthouse

Stony Stratford and Watling Street

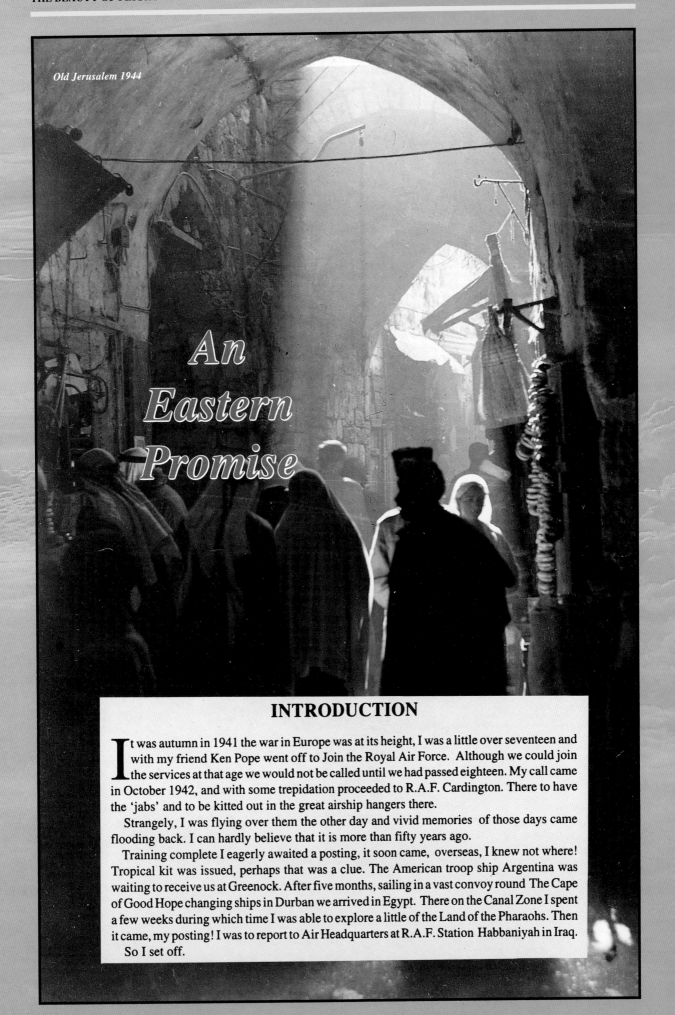

Old Jerusalem 1944

An Eastern Promise

INTRODUCTION

It was autumn in 1941 the war in Europe was at its height, I was a little over seventeen and with my friend Ken Pope went off to Join the Royal Air Force. Although we could join the services at that age we would not be called until we had passed eighteen. My call came in October 1942, and with some trepidation proceeded to R.A.F. Cardington. There to have the 'jabs' and to be kitted out in the great airship hangers there.

Strangely, I was flying over them the other day and vivid memories of those days came flooding back. I can hardly believe that it is more than fifty years ago.

Training complete I eagerly awaited a posting, it soon came, overseas, I knew not where! Tropical kit was issued, perhaps that was a clue. The American troop ship Argentina was waiting to receive us at Greenock. After five months, sailing in a vast convoy round The Cape of Good Hope changing ships in Durban we arrived in Egypt. There on the Canal Zone I spent a few weeks during which time I was able to explore a little of the Land of the Pharaohs. Then it came, my posting! I was to report to Air Headquarters at R.A.F. Station Habbaniyah in Iraq.

So I set off.

The journey to Habbinayah was quite an adventure. The train from Ishmalia sped through the night across the desolate Sinai desert and I dozed. When I awoke there was a broad golden beach edged with a gentle surf, as the train raced along the beach seemed endless. The wide expanse of sea was in the light of a full moon. That was my first sight of the Mediterranean and I have never seen it more beautiful.

THE DESERT BUS

Damascus had changed little for hundreds of years. During the short time there I wandered the ancient streets, bazaars and markets, and walked along the 'Street Called Straight' where tradition has it that St. Paul was converted. Then I was on my way once more. An early morning report to the Nairn Bus Company caused me

Roman Temple, Baalbek

Haifa in those days was the terminal of the oil pipe line from Kirkuk in Iraq, and from high on Mount Carmel the harbour could be seen busy with tankers loading oil to fuel the war effort. I did not know it then but I was to come to know the pipe line well, often patrolling the vast length in an Avro Anson landing at the pumping stations, on just prepared desert strips known as H1, H2, H3. (Haifa Pipe Line, station 1 etc.)

The army truck I climbed into at Haifa followed the coast road past towns I had only heard of in history lessons; Tyre, Siddon and so to Beirut, then a most gracious city. In those days moving about meant taking what transport was available; so with a few dry rations I found myself in a wagon on a freight train, setting off for Damascus. The train climbed up into the mountains, often the bridges were just the width of the track, held high with a tracery of steel. I sat in the open door on the edge of the truck looking down between my feet into the depths of the valley far below. Eventually the train stopped in a grove, then it was a quick dash to the engine to get some hot water to make tea and a wander amongst the trees to pick pomegranates and apricots. The journey continued: we trundled past the Roman Temple at Baalbek and that evening drew into Damascus.

some surprise, for there was a huge articulated bus. It had a massive towing unit with accommodation for the relief crew then behind that a spacious unit, very like an aircraft cabin, with large reclining seats. As we boarded the bus we were given blankets and a packed lunch.

The bus slowly weaved through the narrow packed

The train to Damascus

The Nairn Bus

streets of the town with many a cheerful wave from the crowds of children lining the route. Soon the town gave way to desert. The bus speeded up and the driver followed the double row of old petrol cans which marked the way across what seemed an endless desert all the way to Baghdad. The bus stopped at sunset. It was the time of Ramadan, so the Muslim passengers disembarked, spread their mats on the sand and made their prayers as the sun slipped below the horizon.

Our next stop was in the morning at a rest house at Al Ramadi, a tiny village in the midst of that lonely wilderness. There we enjoyed a breakfast of eggs and chappaties.

On our way again, and after a couple of hours the bus paused at the main gate to R.A.F. Habbaniyah, I saw its famous signpost 'London 3287 miles Baghdad 55 miles'. There I was to stay for the next three years, during which time I travelled on the 'Nairn Desert Bus' several times.

The use of the old cliche 'it's a small world' is common but its meaning is often true. Just a few years ago I was at a dinner party in Brentwood Essex sitting next to a lady previously unknown to me. We talked of various things and eventually I asked her were she came from.

"Beirut," she replied. I asked "Why do you still live there?" It was the time of the recent civil war.

She replied, "I have a house in the mountains which is very lovely, but in any case my money is all there and I cannot bring it out."

We talked of Beirut in its more gracious days and I spoke of my time there during the war and how I had travelled several times to and from Baghdad on the 'Nairn Bus'.

"I am Mrs. Nairn, the widow of the owner," she told me.

How strange that coincidence seated us side by side at that dinner in Brentwood some forty years on.

During my stay at Habbaniyah I travelled about my duties all over the command, which was called 'Paiforce'

'Tiffin' is delivered to the mess

Dawn over New York (c.1930). Note the airship over the river.

The Dornier Do x visits New York (c.1929).

(Persia and Iraq Force). The tide of war had moved away, the base being used mainly as a staging post for India and the far east, especially as the war in Europe was drawing to its conclusion and the forces were being built up for the final assault on Japan.

How I would like to travel once more to some of the places in Iraq, to Ur of the Caldees, Babylon, Ninivah, in Persia, (now Iran) to Hamadan and Isfahan to name a few. Then the desert was harsh, but nevertheless a peaceful, tranquil place; now!!

Dubai, 1944

Habbaniyah: The building in the centre is St. George's Church and the roads are lined with Eucalyptus and Pomegranate.

Iraqi workers with the animal hide floats they used to cross the river Euphrates.

Formation of 'Wapitis' of 600 Squadron.

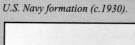

The Junkers 'Flying Wing'. Passengers were accommodated in the wing (c.1930).

U.S. Navy formation (c.1930).

Hawker Hart of 600 Squadron. Flown by Sqadron Leader Robert Faulds (c.1934).

It was at Habbaniyah that I met Jim Dunbar, we became friends but were posted in different directions, losing touch until we met up again when Jim's bank moved him to London in 1968 and he came to live at Thorpe Bay near Southend Airport where I was Chief Flying Instructor.

Jim was a trustee manager with the Natwest bank in the City of London, specialising in trusts and estates. So it was natural that when his uncle died Jim's aunt asked him to administer the estate. His uncle was Group Captain Stuart commanding officer of '600' City of London Squadron R.A.F. with a keen interest in photography. Jim asked me to go with him to the house in Pinner.

There was an interesting collection of cameras which I was able to purchase from the estate, and I still have a miniature 'spy camera' which was part of the group. But by far the most interesting were the early photographic glass negatives I found. On examining the first couple I realised it was a treasure. The first picture was of a formation of 'Wapitis' in flight and the next a shot of London taken from 5500 ft. in April 1934. The River Thames flowed through the centre dotted with ships and barges, for the river was used for commercial traffic beyond Westminster Bridge in those days. The lines of the main roads were prominent. The South Bank was as yet undeveloped and dominated by County Hall. When flying above the City now it is difficult to pinpoint Wren's Church of St. Bride, with a steeple like a bride cake; it is just off Fleet Street but now surrounded by taller buildings. St. Paul's Cathedral also merges with its surroundings, yet in that early picture our City is dominated by the majestic Cathedral: just as Sir Christopher Wren intended.

I questioned Auntie.

"Are there any more of these glass plates Aunt Jean?"

She replied, "There were thousands but I did not think they were any use so I threw them away." There were also negatives taken in New York in the year 1929: of which the 'Dornier DoX' flying boat are very spectacular, but for me the most evocative is the tiny biplane flying close to a cumulonimbus (thunder) cloud above a snow capped mountain. The weather must have been bitter, I expect the photographer in the other aircraft, likely to have been an open cockpit biplane like the other, had frozen fingers and stinging eyes. It needs a lot of skill to fly such an aircraft, yet here they are above snow capped mountains, flying close to a cloud which can produce the most dangerous turbulence and one posing for the other. The photographer has produced a perfect composition and the tiny aircraft is silhouetted against the only light pieces of cloud: superb, I wish *I* had taken it.

Open cockpit biplane close to the storm, above the mountains of Scotland.

A Flight into Renaissance Italy

Apuan Alps, Tuscany

Nino checked the approach. It was clear, so he lined up on the runway and pressed the radio transmit button. "Romeo Juliet (that was our call sign) is ready for departure," he said.

"Romeo Juliet is clear for take off, the surface wind, two five zero degrees at seven knots," came the reply,

As Nino opened the throttle he responded, "Romeo Juliet, roger" (in aviation 'roger' means, I have received all your last message.) Twenty, thirty, forty knots: we accelerated along the short grass runway at Cinquale:

sixty knots; then Nino eased back the control column and we were airborne.

Our flight was to take us into the Apuan Alps, to quarries high in the mountains from where the famous Carrara marble has been hewn since ancient times. The Tuscan day was hot, the aircraft was heavy and its performance low, so our route was to take us along the coast to gain height, then back along the valley and into the mountains and the quarries a few miles behind the marble town of Carrara.

A marble quarry in the Apuan Alps.

Holes drilled in stone ready for wooden pegs. Aswan, Egypt.

Carrara developed from the Roman village of Kar (Kar was a pre Roman word for stone) and stone has been quarried from high in the mountains behind the town for over two thousand years.

In those distant times the great blocks were torn from the mountainside just as queen Hatshepsut's masons cut massive granite blocks from a quarry at Aswan, Egypt. There they were shaped into obelisks before being rafted down the Nile to adorn the Temple of Amun at Karnak. The Egyptians drilled a line of holes in the stone and forced in wooden pegs which would then be soaked with water. This caused the wood to expand with sufficient force to split the stone with a mighty crack.

The same method was used at Carrara: quarrymen would look for a natural split in the marble and drive in iron wedges until the stone yawned open. Then wooden blocks would be forced into the crevices and soaked with water; in time came a sound like thunder as the swelling wood split a massive block from the mountain and it would tumble onto the quarry floor, often breaking into smaller pieces. This method was used until 1858 when a steel cable driven by a motor revolutionised the cutting. This made it possible to produce the regular shaped blocks just as we see today, and these are much easier to work.

THE TUSCAN COAST

A regiment of umbrellas at Viareggio.

Soon after take off we were over the beach. In tranquil contrast to the stark mountains behind, the sand sloped gently to the sea. Like a parade of guards, umbrellas of many colours, in regimental rows disappeared into the distance. We climbed slowly as we flew along the coast often acknowledging with a 'wiggle' of our wings the greeting from the holiday makers below.

As the multitude of umbrellas came to an end, there, fifteen hundred feet below was Viareggio, a noted resort with all the attractions of a seaside holiday town. I had been there a number of times, but for the first time saw the busy commercial port which was set out below with its busy shipyard and several vessels under construction on the docks.

The shipyard at Viareggio.

Chianti vineyards, Tuscany.

GIACOMO PUCCINI

A little higher, a little further, and slightly inland was a serene lake, Lake Massaciuccoli was beloved by the famous opera composer Giacomo Puccini who made his home by its shore in the tiny town of Torre del Largo (the Tower by the Lake) and composed many of his operas overlooking the lake and the mountains beyond. As we looked down on this beautiful August afternoon we could see Torre del Largo, Puccini's Villa, and the piazza where a statue of the Maestro looks out over his lake. The open air theatre was being prepared for the evening performance of his first opera 'Le Villi', for now was the time of the Puccini Festival.

Torre del Largo, Puccini's home.

An evening performance of 'Le Villi', the ballet scene.

LUCCA

Nino had been an Italian Air Force pilot, and he handled the aircraft with the skill one would expect of such a man. He gently banked to the left to turn inland with the smooth control which is another important attribute of a good pilot. Soon there was Lucca! The visual impact of Lucca from our privileged position was extraordinary, for there spread out was a perfect mediaeval town, still surrounded with a complete defensive wall, making it appear like an island, encompassed by a sea of green which was the surrounding moat and grass area. Cathe-dral and churches with superb marble facades were set out below, often in spaces echoing shapes from the Roman period. The 12th century church of San Michele in Foro dominates the square which was once the Roman Forum; while nearby were houses built in the Middle Ages built on the foundations of the Roman Amphi-theatre which had stood there in the second century.

We looked down into the Piazza dell Anfiteatro and imagined the vast arena filled with wild animals and gladiators fighting to the death, spurred on by the cheers of thousands of spectators who filled the vast terraces.

Above: Medieval Lucca,.

Left: The Piazza and Church of St. Michele.

PINNOCHIO

Reluctantly we turned away from Lucca, soon to pass over the magnificent terraced garden (*c. 1650*) of Villa Garzoni at Collodi. It was in the kitchen of the castle here during the long winter evenings that Pinnochio was 'born'. Turning north and continuing the climb along the valley, we flew by numerous hilltop villages for which Tuscany is famous. Our track took the aircraft over the city of Barga contained by its perimeter wall and dominated by the church set on the highest part of the hill, on which medieval Barga stands. Today Barga looked quite tiny, several thousand feet below as we turned west into the mountains.

The terraced gardens of Villa Garzoni, Collodi.

INTO THE MOUNTAINS

Nino gently weaved the aircraft between the peaks towering above and peppered with clouds. Then we came to the quarries. "That one is where the marble came from for Michelangelo's *Pieta*," exclaimed Nino. Quarrymen were still at their dangerous work, cutting the vast blocks of marble at the very edge of the mountainside. Michelangelo made many trips to the mountain quarries during his eighty eight years of life, and several times runaway blocks nearly brought him to a tragic, premature end. The very best marble known as 'statuario' comes from this area. So it was that the master made the dangerous journey into the mountains to select his own blocks. They had to be the finest whitest marble, without veins, fractures or flaws of any kind. Having selected the piece, usually weighing twenty to thirty tons, it then had to be moved down the mountain face to the ox-carts waiting below.

From this quarry Michelangelo obtained the marble for his 'Pietà', now in St. Peter's, Rome.

BRINGING THE MARBLE
DOWN THE MOUNTAIN.

Narrow pathways known as 'zizze' were constructed. The 'zizze' zigzagged their way down the precipitous mountainside. The surface of the 'zizze' was made of roughly packed stone, and wooden stocks were driven into the rock on each side. The huge blocks, powered by gravity, slid down on soaped timbers which were placed across the path in front of the blocks while the movement was restrained by thick hemp ropes turned around the stocks embedded in the rock on each side of the path. The work crews descended slowly, moving rollers from the rear to the front as the marble rolled on, whilst other workers shifted restraining ropes from one group of stocks to the next. The great ropes and the steel cables which replaced them towards the end of the last century were not totally reliable; sometimes a block would break free with tragic consequences. Now huge lorries loaded with immense blocks make their tortuous way down the zigzag paths used of old. The marble ends that part of its journey in the yards of Carrara, where the masons cut it into the required shapes and sizes to be distributed all over the world.

We spent about half an hour in the peaks enjoying the splendid mountainscapes and viewing several other of the quarries, of which there are about two hundred. Then it was time to return to Cinquale. Nino reduced the power

Bringing down the marble, today.

and the aircraft went into a gentle descent, flying down and weaving with the twists and turns of the valley until we came to the seaside plain with the airfield a mile ahead.

BACK TO CINQUALE

A further reduction of power and we skimmed the trees at the airfield boundary. Then we were over the runway: gently back with the control column, power off, and the aircraft touched down, slowed, then turned for the club-house. So we came to rest at the end of one of the most interesting flights I have ever experienced.

Medieval workers toiling with a vast marble block. Painting: Peter Froste.

Michelangelo.

A mountain yields its marble
The sculpture gently moulds,
With loving care, from silken rock
A human shape unfolds.

Driven by great passion
With genius born of strife
With roughened hands he does his work
And scriptures come to life.

Jackie Stock.

The Emerging Slave. An unfinished work. Accademia, Florence.

FLORENCE AND MICHELANGELO

The next day I went to Florence. There, in the museum of the Cathedral, I was able to admire Michelangelo's last work, 'The Deposition of Christ'. My final visit was to the Accademia which houses the colossal statue of David 'Il Gigante' (The Giant)" executed by Michelangelo when he was only twenty eight years old, between 1501- 1503. Entering the Accademia one sees on each side of the gallery a series of unfinished works intended for the tomb of Pope Julius II. These give a wonderful insight into the creation of a masterpiece. 'The Slave' in one unfinished piece seems to be struggling to be free of the marble rock which imprisons him.

MICHELANGELO'S DAVID

David stands alone at the end of the building, lighted from above. The life Michelangelo gave to this masterpiece is enhanced by the glow of the light from within. Marble is translucent, and light penetrates the first few inches, is refracted and returns, producing a soft warm glow as if the stone were alive! No other stone has this beautiful quality. Marble from the Apuan Alps has been quarried from ancient times and works created from it can be seen all over the world. The buildings in Roman towns were encased in it, the great cathedrals and churches of the 12th and 13th centuries were faced with it.

Marble of different colours covers the Campanile (Bell Tower) in Florence described by Longfellow as 'The lily of Florence blossoming in stone'. London's Marble Arch was created with it, as was the floor of St. Paul's Cathedral. But there is no doubt that the heyday was during the renaissance when Michelangelo together with some of his contemporaries created so many masterpieces from the incomparable marble of Carrara.

Michelangelo's 'David'. The Accademia, Florence.

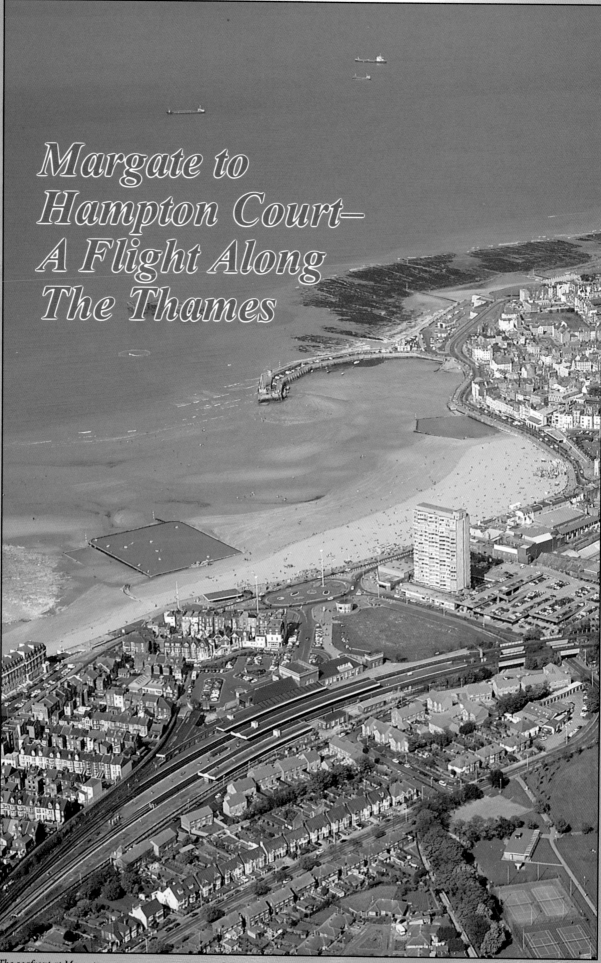

Margate to Hampton Court— A Flight Along The Thames

The seafront at Margate.

Flying back from Ostend, the route tracks the radio beacon from Costa in Belgium to a similar beacon (a V.O.R.) at London, Heathrow. At night when the visibility is good, on the climb out from Ostend and taking up a westerly heading, the lights of Kent and beyond as far as the Essex Clacton coast, some fifty or sixty miles away, can be clearly seen. Looking north, the lights of the towns which line the edge of the sea from Ostend are visible as far as Amsterdam; while in the other direction the ports of Dunkerque, Calais and Boulogne mark the coast of France. The Channel narrows to the west to form the Straights of Dover, where is seems, Cap Gris Ney is reaching out for England. The sea is dotted with the lights of the ships making their way through this, the busiest waterway in the world.

I pressed the transmit button and called, "Kent Radar, this is Bravo Mike" (it is necessary to establish contact on the R.T.- Radio Telephony, before having a conversation).

"Bravo Mike, this is Kent Radar, go ahead"

"Kent Radar, Bravo Mike requests descent and a turn or two around Canterbury"

"Bravo Mike, this is Kent Radar, approved, enjoy yourself!"

Canterbury was so attractive at the lower level, we made a couple of turns round the town, most of it in shadow the low sun just lighting the Cathedral and the tops of the taller buildings. With permission from Kent, I flew on to Leeds Castle, said by Lord Conway to be "the most beautiful castle in the world": my passengers were

The Dunkerque beaches.

Flying at 4500 ft. The continent fades in the distance and the shape of Kent begins to reveal itself, coming to a headland at the North Foreland, with Margate the first town on the North Coast and Ramsgate to the South. Between the two is R.A.F. Manston the home of 'Kent Radar' the service which 'looks after' aircraft between Southend, Kent and the continental seaboard in that area.

I remember once, flying back across Kent in an 'Aztec' 'Bravo Mike' (the aircraft's radio call sign). It was a beautiful evening, the cathedral at Canterbury looking gorgeous, touched as it was by a setting September sun. So I thought perhaps my passengers would like a closer look.

enthralled. However, my daughter Deborah awaiting our return at Southend Airport was getting concerned, so she telephoned 'Kent Radar':

"Hello, have you any news of Bravo Mike?" she asked.

"Yes, don't worry," came the reply, "your Dad's enjoying a sightseeing tour of Kent." So the flight continued, following the 'radio beam' which in turn parallels the North Kent coast until by the Isle of Sheppey, the lights of Shoeburyness shine through the darkness to the left and with Southend to the Right. Now flying between the land masses Kent and Essex we were following the river which for many years has been the great highway for invaders and traders into London and beyond. The familiar voice of the Southend approach controller gives us our instructions and we slide down the glide path for a landing after another memorable flight.

THE RIVER THAMES, ORIGINS.

The Thames, in common with many other rivers of similar name, had its name derived from an ancient word tamus, meaning 'darkness'. The rivers which move over soil tend to become cloudy, or dark, while those flowing down chalk hills become clear running streams.

It would seem then that the name 'Old Father Thames'

changed, so did the course of the river, at one time it flowed as far north as St. Albans. Sometimes the Thames estuary was broad, more like a delta. It is thought that the wide River Blackwater and also the River Crouch may have been part of The Thames.

Gentle tilting of the landmass towards the south encouraged the river to move its course from the Vale of St Albans until it found the easiest route, through Essex. At the same time the tilting combined with the relentless pounding of the North Sea's tidal surges eroded the land, creating a gap which we now call The Straights of Dover. Britain was now an island and the Thames a river, with its estuary into The North Sea.

Kent, The English Channel, Cap Gris Ney and the French Coast.

contains a lot of truth, for it was flowing some 30 million years ago. Then, massive upheavals formed the mighty Alps, and the ripples reached the chalklands of the Thames valley, flints formed in the chalk providing early man with a material which could be fashioned into tools and weapons, so helping to make man master of the Thames Valley.

Even in its early days the Thames rose in what we now call the Cotswolds. Britain was still connected to the continent and the Thames a tributary of the Rhine. Time passed: ice ages came and went, interspersed with warm periods. These caused the river to rise and fall. Sometimes its flow was slow and it deposited gravels on the flood plain. Other times, when the sea was low, it would flow faster and cut a deeper valley. As the landscape

A FLIGHT ALONG THE RIVER THAMES.

The day has dawned bright and clear, south-east England is under the influence of a high pressure system, the gently descending air keeps the sky cloud free and the wind light. Perhaps as the sun gets a little higher fair weather cumulous will form and that will be nice for it is very photogenic and will enhance our pictures. Since that night flight there has been a continued decline of commercial air traffic between Essex, Kent and the continent, 'Kent Radar' has closed, the controlled airspace known as 'the cross channel special rules zone' no longer exists. So now once clear of Southend we can fly where we like without talking to anyone; that's how I like to fly.

I am not sure if the Thames Estuary really starts at the

North Foreland but that is where we will start our flight. The 'Cessna' is re-fuelled and a preflight inspection is complete, the engine started and the aircraft receives clearance to holding point 'Charlie' for 'runway 24'. (a runway pointing 240° from north). There preflight engine and airframe checks are completed and we make a call to air traffic:

"Southend Lima-Whisky is ready for departure"

"Lima-Whisky is clear to line up"

"Lima-Whisky is clear to take off with a left turn out to leave the zone at 1500 feet, the surface wind 230°10 knots".

"Southend Lima-Whisky is clear to take off with left turn to leave the zone at 1500 feet" (all instructions are required to be acknowledged). As we get airborne and turn left, the town of Southend is spread out below, soon we are approaching the Isle of Sheppey, here we can say goodbye to Southend and cross Kent to Ramsgate where we will start our flying exploration of the River Thames.

50th Anniversary of Dunkerque. The 'Little Ships' escorted by HMS Alacrity.

Ramsgate.

From Ramsgate on the south Kent coast around the Foreland past Margate and as far as the Isle of Sheppey the coast has largely escaped the desecration of riverside industrial development, a plight which our river has suffered on both banks from Sheerness on the Kent side and Canvey Island on the north shore as far as London.

RIGHTLY CALLED "KENT'S LEISURE COAST"

The eastern tip of Kent is so narrow that the towns of Ramsgate to the south and Margate to the north might even be regarded as twins but there the similarity ends.

RAMSGATE.

The North Foreland.

Ramsgate has its origins in Roman times, developing into a fishing village and coming to the height of its prosperity with the building of the harbour which was constructed by order of Parliament in 1749. Thereafter the fishing fleet grew until the fleet was the largest on the south coast, boasting 144 vessels. From the first world war the fishing industry went into decline, but the little town with its fine harbour was yet to achieve its most famous task. In the second world war during the evacuation from Dunkerque over 42,000 troops were landed at Ramsgate. A memory of that epic is captured in the fishing boat, still moored in the harbour, which came back through those war torn seas with 130 troops. Subsequently the harbour went into decline but the last ten years has brought a change. Ferries run from Ramsgate now, the harbour is a fine marina, nearby a museum depicts Ramsgate's maritime history while in a dry dock rests the steam tug, Cervia. Built in 1946 it spent most of its life moving ocean liners in and out of the Port of Tilbury.

MARGATE

In vivid contrast, just across the peninsula, stands Margate, a town more dedicated to pleasure. This south east corner of England probably has the best sunshine record, with sandy beaches, secluded bays and a sea which is safe for swimming. Near the main beach, covering many acres, is 'Dreamland', a pleasure park dominated by a giant ferris wheel and the country's largest 'big dipper'. However, there is much more of interest in this town whose origins go back to the Roman period and beyond. It has been suggested that Margate's popularity as a resort started when people flocked to the town to attend auctions of smuggled goods. Smugglers brought contraband ashore often hiding it, and themselves, in the caves which riddle the cliffs. Some were caught; they would then be incarcerated in the Old Police Station and eventually the confiscated goods sold. The bargains to be had attracted throngs of visitors. Now, a visit to the Old Police Station and Margate's Caves can be an evocative experience of those 18th and 19th century days when, from the old coastguard station, the Preventive Forces would set forth in an attempt to intercept the illicit spirits being brought ashore.

THE GROTTO

*"Men sometimes overlook the thing
under their very feet".*
R. Sabatini.

In 1835 some schoolboys playing in fields adjacent to their school dislodged a tablet of stone revealing the circular opening into a dome; after unknown years, they were looking down into 'The Shell Temple'. Hidden from time immemorial, the Grotto's origin and purpose

'Dreamland', Margate.

are still very much a mystery, although H.G. Wells believed 'The Shell Temple' pre-dates the Roman invasion by thousands of years. Howard Bridgewater's theory suggests the Grotto is of Phoenician Origin, c100 BC. This Grotto which is unique in the world consists of an entrance passage, a circular Rotunda, a Serpentine Passage with an Altar Chamber at the end. It is decorated throughout with a delicate tracery of shells. Nowhere is the Cross to be seen but the designs reveal the Egyptian Ankh, (their ancient symbol of life), Bacchus, the Roman God of wine, with bunches of grapes, together with phallic signs, snakes and flowers.

A Victorian novelist described the Shell Temple at Margate as "The Eighth Wonder of the World."

The Shell Grotto, The Serpentine Passage.

The Shell Grotto, The Altar Chamber.

The Shell Grotto, The Dome.

RECULVER: ROMAN REGUBIUM.

Flying west, the built up area of Margate and Westgate, with their cliffs and bays, gives way to a straight flat coast at the end of which is Reculver and the remains of a Roman Fort. Regubium (the Roman name) was one of a series known as 'The Forts of The Saxon Shore'. In the third century AD. the Romans built a number of forts round the coast of south east England, to keep the Saxon and Viking invaders at bay. Regubium was one. Not much now remains, only a few remnants of the outer wall which still display the distinctive rectangular shape of a Roman fort. The Romans abandoned the British Isles in 403 AD. and the mighty forts fell into decay, eventu-

into the country, then came airpower! During the first world war the silver reflections of the moon and stars guided the Zeppelins, while in the second world war the river pointed the way for huge formations of Nazi bombers, like a radio beam today, to the vast port of London.

So, just as in Roman times forts came to be built; but this time they were way out in the estuary. These complexes of steel platforms interconnected with walkways housed anti aircraft units. They must have been desolate posting for soldiers; especially in the depth of winter.

They can still be seen, starkly silhouetted against the sky from Regubium.

Reculver. The remains of the Roman walls and the twin towers of St. Mary's can be seen.

ally the remains were occupied by the very Saxons they were built to keep out. At Regubium a church was constructed within the Roman walls, but with the passage of time the church went through many rebuildings until in the 18th century, St. Mary's came to be built. St Mary's had two very distinctive towers and for many years local seafarers used them as an aid to navigation. Finally, there came the time when the church was to be demolished, the sailors made so many protests at the threatened loss of their navigation aid that the towers were reprieved. There they remain today still guiding little ships safely along the river.

WORLD WAR II FORTS.

The River Thames was the great highway for travellers, traders and invaders for 'donkey's years'. Until this century they were borne by the waters of the river, deep

HERNE BAY AND WHITSTABLE.

Now it takes but a few minutes to fly the miles from Margate to Whitstable, in the seventh century most people walked, following 'The Saxon Shore Way', parts of which still exist. This ancient footpath follows the coast from Rye in the south for 147 miles to Dartford in the north. Herne Bay is mainly a residential area with a lovely walk along the low lying cliffs following the Saxon Shore Way back to Regubium, while following the Saxon Shore Way to the west for about six miles is Whitstable.

The Romans knew about the good things of life and it was here, at Whitstable, they came for oysters. The little port has been famous since those days and even now the dredgers are often at work gathering oysters, known as 'Royal Whitstable Natives'. By now we can see across the River Swale, from where it joins the Thames, to the Isle Of Sheppey.

THE RIVER SWALE AND THE ISLE OF SHEPPEY.

The Isle of Sheppey is bounded by the Thames on the north shore, the River Medway to the west and to the south in a sweeping crescent from Whitstable to Sheerness is the River Swale. Perhaps it is this separation from the mainland which gives Sheppey its very lonely character. There is only one town of note, at the western end, the port of Sheerness. On the mainland the Saxon Shore Way meanders along the seashore, while in striking contrast, the Roman Watling Street (now the A2) is still

a boat ride along the Swale Coastline which provides a unique way to appreciate the parts which cannot be reached any other way.

With luck, you will see the red sails, borne aloft on an 80 foot mast, creating the distinctive shape of a Thames barge as it moves slowly along the Swale. A number of these have been lovingly restored and now grace our east coast rivers.

Henry VIII loved the remoteness of the island so much that he even honeymooned there. Those sands are still there for visitors to appreciate today; even at the eastern end at Shellness there is a beach reserved for Naturists.

*The Isle of Sheppey and the river Swale (looking east). Inset: Oyster Catchers. Photo: **Gerry Downy**.*

as straight as the builders constructed it, a straightness which is emphasised at night when flying above, by the lights of thousands of cars. In Roman times the legions marched from the ports of Regubium (Reculver) and Dubrae (Dover) for Londinium (London). In the places where they stopped for rest and entertainment settlements began and grew into the bustling towns of today. Where Watling Street crossed the rivers, especially the Medway at Durobrivae (Rochester) encampments were built to protect the crossings. In Chaucer's time pilgrims followed the road, stopping to tell their tales at the inns, so for two thousand years the road has been used by rich and poor, merchants and kings. Apart from the Saxon Shore Way, a long distance footpath, each bank of the River Swale is without roads, so it remains very unspoiled. A home for many thousands of seabirds and waders which live on the lonely beaches and the several nature reserves. The best way to enjoy all this is to take

Isle of Sheppey Prison

Medway Marine (aerodrome). Inset: The red sails of the Thames barges.

ROCHESTER AND CHATHAM

The historic town of Rochester has an awesome castle surrounded with medieval battlements and from where, atop England's finest Norman keep, there are splendid views over the River Medway. Looking the other way, just beyond the castle moat is Rochester Cathedral. The origins of the Cathedral go back to Saxon times when it was founded by King Ethelbert. It was then a simple building, but later it gave way to the splendid Norman Cathedral we see today. Charles Dickens lived in Rochester for many years and the 'Charles Dickens Centre' is housed in the splendid 16th century Eastgate House. There you can 'meet and listen' to the characters from his novels, then afterwards walk the streets past the houses and inns those very people used. Watling Street, the main Roman Road to and from London and the Kent ports must have been adequate for the legions. The Romans constructed defences where Watling Street crossed the Medway. Later Henry I built the great Castle there: the road was then used by Chaucer's pilgrims. They paused in Rochester and the Canon told The Yeoman's Tale.

It was only with the advent of the motor car when the road, and especially the Medway crossing at Rochester, became inadequate after almost two thousand years. The M2 was constructed. Now travellers speed round the Kent towns on their way to the channel ports.

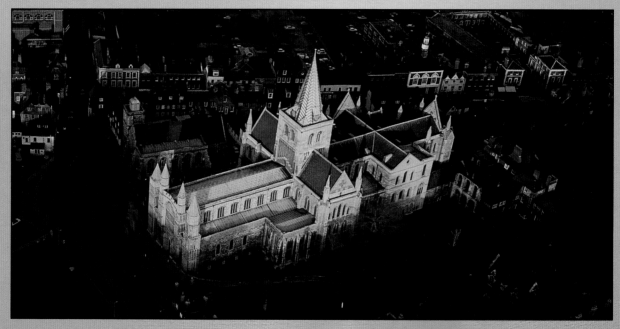

Rochester Cathedral, touched by a September sun.

SHORT BROS. AND THE FLYING BOATS

'Shorts', a famous name in aviation, had their factory in Rochester, close by the river. There they built the beautiful Empire 'C' class Flying Boats during the 1930's. These wonderful aircraft opened the skies to the far flung parts of what was the British Empire. They all had a name beginning with 'C'; 'Canopus' was the first, (launched at Rochester in 1936 and made its first flight on 3 July). I was fortunate to fly in 'Canopus' from Bahrain to Lake Habbaniyah near Baghdad. Once, when crossing the Jordanian desert the pilot of 'Cleopatra' (went into service with BOAC on the Poole-Karachi route, 21st May 1940) saw the R.A.F. convoy at rest, came down low, circled, then gave us a 'slow fly past'. I hope it was

CHATHAM

Chatham is so close to Rochester that it might even be considered a twin. In medieval times Chatham was a tiny unknown village, then Henry VIII created a naval dockyard there. It was further developed by his daughter Elizabeth I and so it remained, growing in importance until it was closed in 1984 soon after its last major naval role, refitting nuclear submarines. Between Henry and the submarines The Royal Naval Dockyard served this island Kingdom well. There was a fracas when a Dutch fleet under Admiral von Ruyter, to the astonished and horrified gaze of onlookers from the shore, crashed through the chain boom guarding Chatham and destroyed four ships of the line. The first ship to be built in

RAF convoy rests in the Jordanian Desert and 'Cleopatra' circles then departs with a 'slow fly past'. Painting by Ron Slade.

as much a thrill for the passengers as it was for us around our campfires in that vast desert. (In those days flying was a far more relaxed, uncontrolled experience). 1939 came and with it the war, the 'C' class flying boat design was developed into a warplane, the Sunderland was born. Hundreds slid down the slipway into the Medway, took off from 'Medway Marine' and went to war. On a modern aviation chart, by Rochester in the Medway, a symbol of a circle can be seen with an anchor in the centre, that is the site of 'Medway Marine' an active 'airfield'. Only once in the many years flying in the area have I been told over the RT. (Radio telephony) "be advised, Medway Marine is active," but even then I did not see a flying boat or seaplane, arriving or departing.

the new dockyard at Chatham was the Sunne, a pinnice of 56 tons. There followed some 500 ships perhaps the most famous being H.M.S. Victory. She was laid down at Chatham in 1759, commissioned in 1778, fought and was Nelson's flagship at the Battle of Trafalgar in 1805.

Today you can walk the decks of H.M.S. Victory at Portsmouth, admire the work of the Kent craftsman who built this great wooden walled ship, wonder at the skill of the seamen who sailed H.M.S. Victory and the courage of the men who manned the vast cannons in the confined gundeck. H.M.S. Victory is still in commission and is flagship of Commander-in-Chief, home command. Nearby in a purpose built museum is Henry VIII's flagship Mary Rose, recently recovered from her muddy resting place in The Solent.

The Docks at Chatham, filled once again with sailing ships celebrating 'A Parade of Sail'.

Today the Royal Naval Dockyard at Chatham has been preserved as a time capsule from the Georgian age of sail. Here you can walk though the dockyard which created those 500 great ships, see the buildings which made the various components, the masts, the sails the ropes etc., which were then brought together in the building slips, until, at last another ship slid into the waters of the Medway.

River Medway

THE RICHARD MONTGOMERY
A BOMB FILLED WRECK

As ships have had to do since the second world war, they have to separate as they pass The Isle of Sheppey, those for the Medway ports moving closer to the Kent shore and those for Tilbury and London move a bit towards Essex. For there off Sheerness is the wreck of the Richard Montgomery. This ship filled with bombs and ammunition swung while at anchor in 1944, hit a sand bank, and there she has been ever since. Laden as the Montgomery still is with 3,173 tons of bombs, the ship is quite a problem. She lies only 200 yards from a main shipping

shipping and the nearby towns. A menace which becomes visible each low tide as the superstructure appears above the water.

BEYOND THE MEDWAY

Where the Medway flows into the Thames the Essex coast moves closer and although six miles separates the two land masses, it is here that the Thames Estuary begins. Now we will have to look on each side of the river to enjoy our flight towards London.

To the right is Shoeburyness (the word ness means

The wreck of the Richard Montgomery. Inset: Ferry Olau 'Hollandia' at Sheerness.

lane, two miles from Sheerness and three from an oil refinery. It is thought that if the Montgomery 'went up' it would provide one of the biggest non-nuclear explosions in history. The 'official line' on the Montgomery is that old age and sea water are gradually rendering the bombs harmless, but other opinion considers the explosives more unstable and therefore more difficult to handle safely. Something will have to be done one day; in the meantime this 'time-bomb' rests off Sheerness, surrounded with red buoys, a menace to

headland or cape) and close by, the vast lonely Maplin Sands, an area we can seldom fly over as it is designated a 'danger area'. Here the Ministry of Defence 'play' with their guns and often the nearby houses are rocked by their thunder. There was once a plan to build London's third airport there but after a little preliminary work, the scheme was abandoned for cost. So the seabirds still have their home there and the sands yield their cockles to the fishermen from Leigh.

Crop mark of a Bronze Age Camp, with irregular crop marks formed in the ice age, known as 'ice wedge polygons'.

Thorpe Bay and Shoeburyness

Southend from Canvey Island, with the Ray Gut (a boat channel).

At Shoebury there was an extensive Romano-British settlement and many archaelogical finds have been made. Later, a Danish Fort stood on the site now occupied by the modern barracks.

A little further west is Thorpe Bay, a sought after residential area. It was an 'estate' too in ancient times, because by a fresh water lagoon, later to be engulfed by the sea, stood a Bronze Age village (c.700-1000BC.) In mid summer, just a mile or two north of Thorpe Bay, as the crops are ripening a double huge rectangular mark appears in a field, this crop-mark is evidence of Bronze Age people building an enclosure there, perhaps for defence. An entrance can be clearly seen together with a round house. Interestingly, the field is also covered with irregular marks, these are known as 'ice wedge polygons'. They were formed when water seeped into cracks in the ground, froze and expanded. Later when the ice melted the crevices filled with more fertile material. Now when a crop is grown on the field, it grows differently, shorter, taller or a different colour above the 'cracks' and we can see the marks created by these differences when flying above. They are sure evidence of the 'ice age' reaching Essex some 12,000 to 14,000 years ago; at least!

SOUTHEND ON SEA

Southend, was once a playground for the Eastenders, with hundreds of coaches setting out from the pubs for a day at the seaside and a plate of cockles; but now the town has much more an industrial base. Its famous pier, a mile and a quarter long reaches across the shallow water and sands to the 'Ray' where the water is deep enough for pleasure steamers to berth. The Golden Mile to the east adjoins Thorpe Bay and to the west elegant esplanades, wide sandy beaches, and pretty gardens join first with Westcliff then Leigh on Sea. Until the coming of the railway (a railway which cuts Leigh on Sea in two) all these places were tiny seaside villages, now they are joined in a continuous urban sprawl.

Southend, Sea Fog (advection fog) over the estuary

CANVEY ISLAND

In Roman times the land which is now Canvey Island was inhabited. There have been many Roman and Iron age (75BC-50AD) finds, especially pottery, to confirm this but the most significant feature to indicate the presence of the Romans are 'Red Hills'. Much research has gone into the formation of some redhills and more than 300 are known; all are close to the sea mainly on saltings. It would seem that the 'Red Hills' are a by-product of salt making, the red colour in the soil occurs when earth is burnt by the fires used in the distillation of the sea water to produce salt.

The land on this eastern tip of the British Isles subsided and much of Canvey Island became flooded. Then in about 1620 and in addition to attacking the fleet at Chatham, the Dutch came to Canvey, their engineers built a seawall and reclaimed the land creating Canvey Island.

This gentle tilting of the landmass into the sea continues to this day, and now most of Canvey is below sea level and protected by a massive wall which encircles it.

The River Thames is usually tranquil, but forty years ago, on the 1st February 1953, a hurricane force north wind drove the spring tide from the north sea down towards Kent. The water was unable to pass the land mass of Kent and that together with a force produced by the rotation of the earth turned the mass of water west along the Thames. It breached the sea wall at Canvey and flooded the Island. Sixty eight people died, most of the inhabitants were made homeless and much of the livestock killed. The devastation was not confined to Canvey Island, in all 307 died, 400 homes were destroyed and 30,000 made homeless.

Canvey recovered from that deluge, the seawall was rebuilt stronger and higher, people returned to rebuild their homes and lives. Now the western end of the island has a natural gas terminal, storing and distributing methane gas from the Sahara. The town is very much an urban sprawl. The eastern end is the holiday area with boats filling the creeks and caravans lining the shores. Two of the Dutch cottages have survived from the 17th century, and one gentleman from the period is often seen and heard off Canvey Point. . .

Canvey Island, the Gas Terminal

*Left: The flood disaster of 1953.
Below: The modern Canvey
protected by the new sea wall.*

Photograph courtesy of the Evening Echo

...THE GHOST OF CANVEY

In brilliant moonlight a sorrowful figure wades ashore, taking long stride across the saltings. This striking figure rises above the wall. Over six feet tall, his long golden hair flows out from a shimmering silver helmet with winged decoration. He is said to wear a leather jerkin and has crossed garters beneath his knees. The Warrior seems to wander aimlessly for a while and then, helmet glinting in the moonlight, he returns to the sea.

*When winter nights are long and chill
   With winds a whistling to a shrill,
Could you be sure of sounds you heard?
   A fox... A cat making overtures!*

*A distant drone of a mournful wail
   Re-kindle thoughts of a sinister tale.
Feet advancing...ere caution...do you dare to see?
   The haggardly apparition that maybe faces thee.*

*The eerie silence cometh down and
   Tickles on the breath of dawn
The touch perhaps of a ghostly hand,
   Or the awesome sound of Viking horn.*

BENFLEET AND HADLEIGH

Hadleigh Ray and Benfleet Creek separate Canvey Island from the mainland, with another small island to the east: this is Two Tree Island, now managed by the Essex Wildlife Trust and is an important sanctuary for wildfowl and waders and especially the Brent Geese which come from Siberia to overwinter and feed off the rich banks of eel grass which is abundant on Leigh Marsh.

Benfleet Creek

You might think the tale of the Viking Ghost fanciful but there are stories of Viking longships lying in Benfleet Creek. Could our handsome warrior have been one of the captains? It is known that the fleet came with Hasten, a Viking Commander about 894AD. A stockade was built and guards left while the main force went on a foray inland. The Danes came and destroyed the camp, killed the defenders and set fire to every ship. During the last century, charred wooden ribs were found deep in the mud of Benfleet Creek!

at night when the flickering light falls on the surrounding country, river and the refinery. Strangely, the name Shellhaven has nothing to do with the oil company Shell but with the shell beach known as Shellhaven which is at the entrance of Shellhaven Creek.

Very often heavily laden barges can be seen being towed along Shellhaven Creek. They are bearing waste from London, much of it noxious to be buried in trenches on the marshes. Essex is very much London's dustbin.

Hadleigh Castle and the Country Park

Hadleigh Castle Country Park abuts Benfleet Creek on the North with a seawall protecting the low-lying marsh from the plundering of the sea. Standing on high ground and dominating the park is Hadleigh Castle. The park is a pastoral landscape of woodland, grazing animals, hedges, streams and ponds with an abundance of wild-life. Wildflowers abound and a gentle climb to the ruins of the Norman Castle will afford superb views of the surrounding countryside and across the estuary into Kent and the North Downs. On a sunny day you might even be lucky enough to see adders basking in the sunshine on the grass by the castle wall.

The western boundary of Canvey Island is Shellhaven Creek, Here the gentle marsh landscape gives way to futuristic towers, spheres and cylinders of the great oil refinery, with flames belching from its tall chimneys giving the complex quite an eerie appearance, especially

Shellhaven Oil Refinery: Firefighters at work on a fire.

THE ISLE OF GRAIN TO CLIFFE

On the other side of the river the industrial complexes are confined to the Isle of Grain. There is again a massive oil refinery with a power station nearby and numerous jetties extending into the Medway. Moving west a landscape of lonely marshes and isolated villages appear.

Slowly through the centuries the landmass has been sinking, so now much of this area is lower than the sea and the sea wall built to protect the land is a dominant feature of these marshes. As the centuries go on the height of the wall has to be increased for the land continues to sink at about one foot every hundred years. The present sea walls were largely created in the 13th Century and have been growing since then. Very often the sea is out of sight from the landward side, its presence suddenly revealed by a giant tanker moving by as if

animals are always to be seen; perhaps you will be lucky and see the seals, dolphin and porpoise which occasionally visit our river.

THE CLIFFE POOLS

At Cliffe adjacent to Cliffe Marshes is a large group of ponds, known as Cliffe Pools. They were created by the extraction of clay but are now slowly being refilled with dredgings from the river. Set by a bend in the river in desolate country the shallow muddy waters provide an excellent habitat for waders, especially in their autumn and winter migrations. The rest of the open water pools is alive with thousands of other wildfowl with the marshland and dykes rich in flora and fauna.

The Cliffe Pools. Inset: Excavations in 1964

through the middle of a field. The sea wall separates the saltings from the extensive fresh water marshes criss-crossed with ditches, and mainly used as pasture.

THE SEA WALL WALK

Following the line of the Saxon Shore way, both the sea and the sea wall pass though marshes made famous in Dicken's 'Great Expectations'. Although constructed to protect the land from an invasion by the sea, the path along the top of the wall provides a walk of unsurpassed interest. It must be one of the loneliest windswept walks within such a short distance from London. There are the vast vistas of the broad estuary, the solitary saltings and marshland. There a wide variety of birdlife, plants and

Nearby, in Roman times there was a river crossing which joined with a road in Essex and as a consequence a settlement grew up where the pools are now. In 1964 I was asked to conduct an underwater survey in the ponds. At that time I was involved in underwater exploration and photography. Sadly the water was much too murky for photography, but it did yield some interesting pieces of pottery and one complete pot from the Roman period. While we were working underwater, the archaeologists were excavating by the edge of the pool. Several skeletons were revealed; it was a Romano-British cemetery. Photographs and measurements were taken, the graves refilled. Today those ancient people still rest beside the Thames and at their home.

COALHOUSE AND SHORNMEAD FORTS

From its previous north south route, The Lower Hope Reach, the Thames narrows and bends on to a westerly direction; a perfect place for defences. So in the mid 16th century, near Cliffe on the south shore Shornmead Fort was built together with Coalhouse Fort on the Essex side. Shornmead Fort is now a ruin, but Coalhouse Fort is in splendid condition. They date back to 1540 when Tudor blockhouses were built there. Standing at such a strategic

of an 18th century fishing village is preserved especially on the river front. The Church of St. George which overlooks the river, is contemporary with the village but no longer in use. It contains the statue of an Indian Princess, Pocohontas. She came to England and was presented at the court of King James. She fell ill and sadly died on the ship, moored off Gravesend, before she could sail for her native Virginia. Now her statue in the gardens of the church is a place of pilgrimage for many American visitors. Gravesend is the headquarters of the Port Of

Gravesend. Inset: The statue of Princess Pocohontas

position on the banks of the Thames, they were rebuilt and strengthened with gun batteries added in 1799, as part of the defences against Napoleon. Further work occurred in 1855 and they achieved their present form in 1860 with their development into a casemate (fortified gun emplacement) forts. Coalhouse is now restored, and heavy guns have been acquired to furnish the emplacements; it is planned to re-enact gun-drills and marching with people dressed in contemporary uniforms. Essex County Council have created a Country Park around the fort and this very attractive area, making a visit a super day out. On the Kent bank, The Saxon Shore Way continues past Cliffe, close to the sea wall by the marshes, near Shornmead Fort and on to Gravesend. At Gravesend the ground becomes higher and the ancient footpath, The Saxon Shore Way, ends.

GRAVESEND AND TILBURY

For the early sailors Gravesend was the first port along the river for incoming vessels and much of the character

London Thames Navigation Service. Here the service provides radar and radio control over shipping from Southend to Northfleet Hope (a stretch of river just west of Gravesend). In the days when the Thames was the highway to London for thousands of ships, the pilots would leave Gravesend to rendezvous with their charges to see them safely to and from London; now the service is still provided although much less busy and always there are a number of pilot boats moored in the river.

For a long time one of the few links with Essex east of Tower Bridge was The Tilbury Gravesend Ferry. On the Essex side the ferry berths at the old Ocean Terminal, here in days gone by 'boat trains' left Liverpool Street Station carrying passengers to Tilbury where the train pulled into the Ocean Terminal.

The passengers completed their formalities, walked up the gangplank onto a great Ocean Liner, then, with bands playing and streamers flying, friends waving and weeping, the ship would edge out into the Thames to sail to a far flung corner of the Empire. Now, apart from the ferry, cruise liners use the terminal and most summers the paddle steamer Waverley calls there as it plies the river once again with trippers just as it did in days long since gone.

Nearby are the docks, a vast facility, once a hive of activity now that action is much reduced, although the container terminal adds a colourful touch.

Just along the river bank to the east is Tilbury Fort, probably the most famous fort along the river. What we see was built between 1670-1683 as a defence against a threat from the French and Dutch: it has a splendid triumphal arch with heavy French inspired carving. However, fortification was first built there when Henry VIII erected a blockhouse (a wooden fortification with ports for defensive fire); something like the original construction at Coalhouse.

WEST OF TILBURY

Both banks of the river are now largely bordered with industrial development, starting with the huge paper mill at Northfleet which has taken up most of the river front. The Thames makes a sharp kink to the north around Swanscombe marshes and in our little aircraft here we must be careful, for towering pylons each side of the river carry high voltage power across. Some years ago a pilot flying in a Beagle Pup thought he would fly between the pylons and under the wires; a daring feat. However, he misjudged the sag in the very heavy cables: the fin of the aircraft hit the cables and the aircraft spun into the river. Nothing was found but a cushion. A few

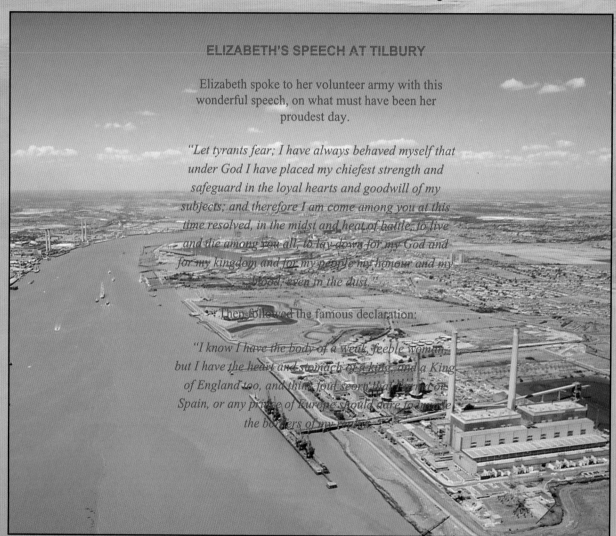

ELIZABETH'S SPEECH AT TILBURY

Elizabeth spoke to her volunteer army with this wonderful speech, on what must have been her proudest day.

"Let tyrants fear; I have always behaved myself that under God I have placed my chiefest strength and safeguard in the loyal hearts and goodwill of my subjects; and therefore I am come among you at this time resolved, in the midst and heat of battle, to live and die among you all, to lay down for my God and for my kingdom and for my people my honour and my blood, even in the dust."

Then followed the famous declaration:

"I know I have the body of a weak, feeble woman, but I have the heart and stomach of a king, and a King of England too, and think foul scorn that Parma or Spain, or any prince of Europe should dare to invade the borders of my realm."

Tilbury, looking west towards London.

QUEEN ELIZABETH AT TILBURY

When the nation was at its greatest peril since the Norman Conquest, and the battle with the Spanish Armada was raging, Queen Elizabeth I came to Tilbury to address and hearten her troops assembled there. She must have been a splendid sight, mounted on a charger, bare headed, her pageboy bearing her white-plumed helmet. Over her bodice she wore a corselet (a piece of armour to cover the trunk) of polished steel. There were just two nobles in attendance, bearing the Sword of State.

days later I was engaged to photograph the damage to the cables: that called for a helicopter. Hovering not more than fifty feet from the cables and quite a way below the top of the pylons I was surprised to see how much damage had been caused to the wires. They looked as thick as an arm and took the full force of the impact. Strangely, although the cables are so thick, partly because the weight causes them to hang low, and partly because of the aircraft's speed, they are difficult to see whilst flying. I am very cautious when flying near them.

Coalhouse Fort.

GREENHITHE

Greenhithe on the Kent shore remains much as it did in the 18th and early 19th centuries; a typical riverside village with a strong feeling for ships and the sea.   Some years ago H.M.S. Worcester, looking very like H.M.S. Victory an 18th century ship of the line, was moored offshore. She was in fact a replica, built in 1906 of steel, not wood, and used as the Thames Nautical College. Then new on-shore college buildings went up, sweeping down to the river's edge and dominating Greenhithe. The new college was born and there was no more need of the Worcester. Sadly in 1978 the ship stripped of non essentials, the great masts truncated, gun ports opened with cannon peeping out she was towed out to Belgium, and scrapped.

H.M.S. Worcester leaving for Belgium.

The Queen Elizabeth II Bridge

EARLY INDUSTRY AT PURFLEET

On both sides of the river, not far from the modern bridge, some 60,000 years ago, Palaeolithic (old stone age) Man occupied the Thames Valley and had a flint tool 'factory' there. Axes were needed to fell trees and to build huts. Flint weapons gave the hunters the power to overcome the wild animals which also made the Thames Valley their home. Mammoth, lion, bear all roamed the fertile lands which edged the river. Flint was easy to work; a nodule of raw flint could be struck, often with a large pebble, the flint would split cleanly, so the flint would be struck again and again until the desired shape was achieved, and a sharp edged axe, arrow head or spear point would emerge from the previous shapeless nodule. In 1965 Susan Palmer found some flint flakes in the Greenlands and Bluelands quarries at Purfleet. Almost 2000 flints at various stages of 'manufacture', from unworked flints (Cores)

The oil terminal at Purfleet. Inset: Excavations at Bluelands quarry in 1965.

through waste chips, to finished tools, hand axes, scrapers, awls and gravers were found. Nearby, Andrew Snelling was working on a contemporary site at Beacon Hill itself, the site of a medieval signal beacon. Very similar finds were made. Now the ancient site is a storage depot for fuel.

THE FORD WORKS

The mighty Ford works takes up the whole of the Thames frontage on the north bank at Dagenham. Established in 1928 the plant was self sufficient. At one time the ore carriers would tie up at the wharf, discharge their cargo which was transferred into Ford's own blast furnace. At the same time the power station was generating electricity to power the assembly lines and at the other end of the factory 60,000 vehicles a year poured out. On the front of the building was a huge and familiar Ford logo, now that has gone, together with the power station and blast furnace, but still cars emerge from the plant.

THE RIVER RODING

The river Roding flows through mid Essex, around Chelmsford and past Abridge, it is bounded by meadows and woods with little boys fishing here and there and occasionally a water mill. A truly pastoral scene. But where the River Roding flows into the Thames it is known as Barking Creek, a name which conjures up a noxious stream. Now that has changed, the east side of the creek still has wharfs and factories where ships still discharge their cargos, mainly timber. To the west there is a disposal works with the Northern Outfall, but now any discharge is clean, and nearby the vast Beckton gasworks has been demolished. Wildlife is returning to the area: skylarks sing at Beckton, goldfinches feed on the thistle, butterflies abound, fish have once again returned to the river.

On the opposite bank all that can be seen from the air are a few earth bunkers. A brass gun foundry was established at Woolwich in 1716, this developed into the Royal Arsenal, which in WWII employed some 40,000 people.

Barking Creek, the River Roding joins the River Thames. The gate-like structure at the entrance is part of the flood defences.

WOOLWICH AND THE ARSENAL

The site of the Arsenal is being developed into a fine housing estate, Thamesmead, and the former Arsenal is remembered in the name of the local football team 'Woolwich Arsenal' and their nickname 'The Gunners'

From now on our flight west along the river is a built up area of continuous interest. Little has come to light of inhabitants prior to the Romans who, in 50AD, had a small town on the northern bank of the Thames at the head of the bridge they had constructed, the site of the present London Bridge. Their town was called Londinium, the name survives in the form of London and the fine Roman town has grown through the centuries into the great city we know today. The city became the hub of an empire covering the world, an empire which flourished on trade, a trade dependent on ships and so London developed into a great port, with many docks.

The largest was the Royal Docks: the first of the group, the Royal Albert Dock was opened in 1880. The Royal Victoria Dock and the King George V Docks were added later. There were three miles of berths from end to end with accommodation for up to fifty ships; usually the berths were full. That is, until recent times and the decline of London as a port. Now the great complex is almost sterile: where once ships were loaded and unloaded with lines of cranes and thousands of dockers; there is London City Airport, handling just a few flights a day to the continent.

Woolwich Ferry

The Royal Docks and Thames Barrier looking east. Inset: The Royal Docks in the 1960's.

THE THAMES BARRIER

Spanning the river by the Royal Docks is the Thames Barrier, one of the wonders of modern times.

'There was last night the greatest tide that was ever remembered in England to have been in this River, all Whitehall having been drowned.'

So wrote Samuel Pepys in his diary for the 7th December 1663.

Central London was again flooded in 1928 with a number of people drowned, and in 1953 came disastrous floods which in particular affected the East Coast and Canvey Island.

GREENWICH

Before the construction of London City Airport, if I was asked for a sight-seeing flight I would often choose to fly along the river from Southend and make a turn or two round Greenwich. Now with the arrival of the City Airport has come an air traffic control zone, which also encompasses Greenwich.

Greenwich is one of my favourite places and must be one of the most beautiful sights in the world, especially from the privileged position above, from a light aeroplane.

Greenwich Park was laid out by Le Notre for Charles II and is a tranquil area with a wooded deer park and a number of exceptionally tame squirrels. It is ground

Thames Barrier with Italian sail training ship Amerigo Vespucci

The menace of the Thames to London has remained from then until the construction of the Thames Barrier. Now when there is a threat from a high tide, or a surge of water caused by a north wind driving the water off the North Sea, south and then into the Thames Estuary, great gates, as tall as a five story building can be raised, and London protected.

which gently rises from the rivers edge and so affords superb views of The Royal Observatory, built by Wren in the park during the 17th century, down to the Queens House and beyond that, by the river's edge, the Royal Naval College, another Wren building.

Like many of the other Thames-side places, Greenwich was once a fishing village which grew after the building of the Palace of Placentia, a favourite haunt of Henry VIII. Little remains of the medieval past at Greenwich, but in 1970 the Grand Square of the Royal Naval College was excavated and the foundations of part of Henry's Palace of Placentia revealed.

The splendour of this magnificent group of buildings set as they are in beautiful parkland with the Royal Naval College fronting the river is witness to both the Royal and Naval past of Greenwich. When Queen Mary decided not to live in The Palace of Placentia she commissioned Christopher Wren to rebuild it as a hospital for aged and disabled seamen. Designed in the Baroque style, the Painted Hall (dining hall) ceiling designed by Thornhill is one of the finest of the period. The hospital was completed in 1705 and a fine chapel was added in 1789. In 1873 the hospital closed and the building became the Royal Naval College.

Greenwich Park, The Royal Observatory, The Queens House and National Maritime Museum, The Royal Naval College, H.M.S. Arkroyal moored in Greenwich Reach and London beyond.

THE CUTTY SARK AND GIPSY MOTH

Close by The Royal Naval College in a dry dock the Cutty Sark is another beautiful reminder of our sea-going traditions. In the 19th century graceful ships like the Cutty Sark, their sails full, raced from the far east around the Cape of Good Hope, looking to be the first home with a cargo of tea. Much smaller and just a short distance away, lies Gypsy Moth, in this fine vessel Sir Francis Chichester circumnavigated the world single handed. It is interesting to note that Sir Francis was first a great airman and his aircraft was a De-Havilland 'Gypsy-Moth'.

Cutty Sark and Gipsy Moth

Greenwich, The Royal Observatory, The Queens House and The Royal Naval College.

Excavations of Henry VIII's Palace of Placentia at Greenwich

The Painted Room (dining hall) of the Royal Naval College, Greenwich designed by Thornhill.

THE QUEENS HOUSE

Just up the sloping lawns from the College is another architectural gem, The Queens House, so called because it was built for Queen Anne of Denmark. In 1614 King James I gave the Palace of Placentia to his extravagant wife, Anne, and she commissioned Inigo Jones to build a villa near the Palace Gatehouse.

As it is we have now a delightful building in the Palladian style. Built in 1618, the house has recently been restored with the aim to return it to something approaching its original form and splendour. It now forms part of The National Maritime Museum.

"The Queen...is building somewhat at Greenwich which must be finished this summer. It is to be some curious device of Inigo Jones, and will cost above 4000li..."

Above: The Great Hall.

Left: The Tulip Staircase.

The Queen's Presence Chamber

The Queen's Bedchamber

THE ROYAL OBSERVATORY

A little further up the slope of the park, through the avenue, past the squirrels at play is the Royal Observatory, not used as such now because both the bright lights and the haze from London rendered it useless. The original Observatory, which still stands amidst a group of early buildings, was built by Wren for Flamsteed, the first Astronomer Royal. Here you can see many of the original astronomical instruments, you can stand astride the zero meridian with one foot in the east and the other in the west, for it is from here that navigation positions east and west are taken. Then, education finished, sit awhile outside and take in the breathtaking view across the park, the Queens House and the Royal Naval College and so to the River Thames where it sweeps in a great 'U' shaped curve around Millwall, forming the Isle of Dogs.

The river by Greenwich is known as Greenwich Reach and often in the reach, abeam Deptford Creek, a visiting ship can be seen moored there; in recent years H.M.S. Ark Royal and the full rigged Italian sail training ship, Amerigo Vespucci, have been there. The ship Amerigo Vespucci is named for the Italian explorer of the same name, and it is after him that the Americas are called.

There are many new buildings on Millwall, now known as 'Docklands' and dominated by Canary Wharf; not many years ago the river and the docks on Millwall would have been busy with ships, tugs and barges. Beyond The Isle of Dogs, to the west, the skyline is punctured by the City of London.

Look carefully, for somewhere in there is St. Paul's Cathedral, however its dome does not dominate the scene now as Wren intended. If the day is clear you will see Tower Bridge, the first bridge across the river in London. The river curves round and in the distance is Westminster Bridge with the Palace of Westminster and Big Ben on the north side behind which is St. James' Park and Buckingham Palace.

In the year 1802, on September the 3rd, William Wordsworth sat upon Westminster bridge and composed the following lines:-

Earth has not anything to show more fair:
   Dull would he be of soul who could pass by
A sight so touching in its majesty
   This city now doth, like a garment, wear
The beauty of the morning; silent, bare,
   Ships, towers, domes, theatres, and temples lie
Open unto the fields, and to the sky;
   All bright and glittering in the smokeless air.
Never did sun more beautifully steep
   in his first splendour, valley, rock, or hill;
Ne'er saw I, never felt, a calm so deep!
   The river glideth at his own sweet will:
Dear God! the very houses seem asleep;
   And all that mighty heart is lying still.

Wordsworth might easily have written that from the high ground at Greenwich park, or even from our privileged position about 1500 feet above the river.

The Royal Observatory, Greenwich Park

London From Greenwich

Docklands (Millwall)

ST. KATHARINE'S HAVEN

Since the decline of commercial activity some of the docks on each side of the river have been changed to become marinas. On the south side, Greenland Dock is now full of leisure craft. But the most imaginative complex is on the north bank, right by Tower Bridge and the Tower of London, is St. Katharine's Haven.

I well remember St. Katharine's Dock from my boyhood, for my father was lock-keeper there. In the 1930's I would be taken to visit the dock especially when a special ship was about to arrive or depart.

I saw Scott's R.R.S. Discovery pass through the lock, and was able to visit her, and later watched as her replacement R.R.S .Discovery II left St .Katharine's at the start of her voyage of exploration. But my most vivid memory of St. Katharine's is from 1940. London was suffering a very heavy air raid and my father had not returned from his duty. About six in the morning I cycled though a blazing East End and City, coaxing my way

Now as we look down we see a superb hotel with a river front promenade and magnificent views along the river and across London. The Ivory House with its distinctive bell tower has been restored and converted, the Dockmasters House has been preserved and still stands at the lock entrance.

The two basins are mainly crammed with 'small ships' although here and there can be seen the tall masts of a Thames Barge and the distinctive shapes of a tug and lightship. It must be wonderful to sail up our historic river and berth right in the centre of London.

Just beyond Tower Bridge stands the Tower of London, a massive castle built by William the Conquerer to protect and control the city. Originally it lay within the Roman city walls but later expansion of the castle eastward, took it beyond the Roman walls.

Part of those Roman walls can be seen within the tower and a fine stretch stands just outside close by Tower Hill underground station. The Romans normally put a course of red tile at regular intervals in a wall, it

St. Katharines Haven and The Tower of London

past firemen and the police until I arrived at the dock. All the warehouses around the eastern basin were ablaze, flammable material had melted and even the water was alight. All was chaos, but dad was alright and he received an award for his rescue work that night. St. Katharine's never recovered from that raid.

both strengthened the wall and helped to keep its shape; now the tile courses distinctly identify construction of the Roman period. There is an interesting walk, quite clearly marked which follows the line of the Roman Wall through the City.

Nearby in a small garden is marked the spot where in

Tudor times the condemned of the nobility were beheaded. At this place Edward IV set up a permanent
scaffold in 1465, and amongst the famous to die there
were, Sir Thomas More, The Earl of Dudley, one time
favourite of Elizabeth, The Duke of Northumberland
and in the late 18th century Lord Lovat who was the last.

LONDON BRIDGE

It is thought that the Romans built the first crossing of
the Thames where London Bridge now stands and, while
there is no firm evidence, it seems most likely. Remains
of a Roman wharf have been unearthed close by the
footings of the present bridge. The first recorded bridge
was a wooden construction built by the Saxons which
was replaced in 1176 by a stone bridge lined on each side
with houses, shops and even a church; it must have
looked very like The Ponte Vecchio (The Old Bridge) in
Florence. Those poor unfortunates, often called
traitors,who had been executed often had their heads
displayed on spikes above the fortified gates at each end.
That bridge was the only river crossing until 1749, now
there are many.

Roman Wall by Tower Hill

London Bridge and The Monument

THE POOL OF LONDON

The Port of London effectively starts at London Bridge and the part of the Thames between the bridge and Limehouse reach is known as the Pool of London. At one time both sides of the river were lined with wharfs with their cranes stretching out over the river as they busily unloaded the ships then refilled them with exports; much as it has happened by London bridge since AD. 30. Now the Pool acts as host to visiting vessels which tie up alongside the Tower of London or by the side of H.M.S. Belfast, a cruiser of WWII, which has a permanent mooring there and is open for a visit. I have even seen one of the beautiful Short Bros. flying boats, a Sandringham, by Tower Bridge. It would have been a wonderful sight to see it land and take off.

THE MONUMENT

On Sunday 2nd September 1666, The Great Fire of London broke out in a baker's shop in Pudding Lane close by London Bridge. St. Paul's and eighty four other churches were destroyed, together with the halls of forty four City Companies. Altogether seven eighths of the City was destroyed in the fire. Of the churches, Wren rebuilt thirty, and they, together with St. Paul's are a reminder of that terrible time and a memorial to the great architect. On a black marble slab covering Sir Christopher Wren's tomb in the crypt of St. Paul's Cathedral is engraved the following inscription:-

The Monument

Lector si monumentum requiris circumspice.

(Reader, if you seek a monument look around you)

Near the place where the great conflagration started, Wren also designed a white column 202 feet high with a cap of guilded flames, which was completed in 1677. The viewing platform near the summit of the 'Fire Monument', affords superb views of the City of London and the River Thames. We now call 'The pillar where the fire began' "The Monument".

St. Paul's Cathedral.

SOUTHWARK AND BANKSIDE

Opposite The Monument on the other bank of the river is
Southwark Cathedral, all that can be seen from the river
is just the top of the Cathedral's four pinnacled towers.
Even from our vantage point about 1,500 feet above the
building it is difficult to define, set as it is now amidst
some tall buildings and near the junction of the railway
lines. The Cathedral remains one of the most impressive
Gothic buildings and is full of interest. The adjacent
river-side was once a pleasure and amusement gardens
and a 16th century 'theatreland' There is known to have
been three theatres here, The Globe, The Swan and The
Rose. The Rose came to light again during some recent
excavations and it is most likely that William Shakespeare played there. The Globe is being rebuilt nearby
much as it was in Shakespeare's time.

The Globe Theatre by the river

Southwark

THE SOUTH BANK

As we follow the river, it bends sharply to the left and
there is the complex of theatres and art galleries, dominated by the Royal Festival Hall. The hall was completed in 1951, the year of the Festival of Britain, which
after the austere war years was wonderful.

The site was largely derelict and the plan was very
imaginative first to build the Royal Festival Hall and use
the rest of the site for a great festival. Then later, when

the festival was over, to develop the rest into a complete
recreation complex along the wonderful river frontage;
a little like medieval Bankside. In those days a shot
tower stood on the site next to the Festival Hall, a great
debate went on about whether to preserve it or not. Alas
it was demolished. A shot tower was used to produce gun
shot. Molten lead was dropped from a measured spoon
from the top of the tower into a bath of water below. The
passage through the air made the lead into a perfect
sphere, and the water cooled it solid. So the lead became

The South Bank with the Festival Hall in 1953. Note the shot tower and Skylon, symbol of the Festival of Britain. Inset: The Festival Hall 1993.

a round shot of the correct size for a pistol or musket.

The views to the north are quite fantastic as we continue on our westerly flight. The tall buildings of the city are dominated by the 'NatWest' tower and in the foreground, Lloyds. St. Paul's is there with its vast dome topped with a gold cross glinting in the sunshine: beyond that are three modern tower blocks that are part of the Barbican complex, rebuilt after the last war. It is an imaginative concept of domestic accommodation but which includes a magnificent concert hall. A barbican was at one time, the outer defences of a city, often associated with a fort. Near the Barbican part of a Roman

fort can be seen, and close by the London Museum a large section of the Roman Wall, again with the distinctive tile courses.

Christopher Wren (also after the great fire) rebuilt St. Bride's Church, the steeple of which towers like a giant 'bride cake' above Fleet Street. The church was badly damaged in 1940 and this produced an opportunity for excavations to take place in the crypt. A Roman house was exposed and is preserved in the crypt and the antiquity of the site as a place of Christian worship was proved, for in the sixth century an Irish Saint from Kildare established a church there.

Left: The Southbank at night.

From our vantage point above the river, the Embankment with its ships gently curves to the south and just past Waterloo Bridge on the plane tree lined promenade is Cleopatra's Needle. Why it is so called I don't know, for this immense obelisk predates that famous queen by about fifteen hundred years and was one of a pair which stood at Heliopolis (sun-city) near present day Cairo in Egypt. A memorial to the R.A.F. stands nearby and on the corner at the start of Westminster Bridge is a statue to the great Warrior Queen of the Belgae, Boudicca, who led the Iron Age Tribe in revolt against the Roman invaders. She fought her last battle against them at Amsbury Banks, lost, and with her daughters committed suicide there. Remains of Amsbury Banks can still be seen in Epping Forest.

Above:
Queen Boudicca, a bronze group of the Queen and her daughters on Victoria Embankment, created in 1850

Left: St Brides.

Below:
City of London, note bomb damaged Natwest Tower & Baltic Exchange.

The Embankment and the River Thames from Vauxhall Bridge looking east.

ABOVE WESTMINSTER BRIDGE

William Wordsworth wrote his poem 'Upon Westminster Bridge' while resting there. I wonder what thoughts he would have penned had he been able to see London as we can from our light aircraft high above the river, but below the flight path of the airliners approaching to land at Heathrow.

Westminster is on the final landing path for 'Runway 28' (that is 280 degrees from north, the approach path is almost westerly). To further assist air traffic control in separation, as we came close to the control zone around London Airport, we were given a 'Squawk', a unique four figure number which we set on the transponder, (a piece of radio equipment about the size of a car radio). As a radar signal from Heathrow hits the aircraft and the transponder aerial, the transponder 'replies' with the number which is set and that, together with our altitude, appear against our 'blip' on the radar screen. As each aircraft has a different number, the controller has positive identification of each 'radar return' together with the altitude of each aircraft.

Westminster Bridge

Below is Westminster Bridge looking to the East, the river bends to the right as it flows past the Embankment. On the left side is The Strand and past that Fleet Street, with the slender 'Bride Cake' spire of St. Bride's, the tallest of Wren's spires reaching Heavenwards. St Paul's stands, barely visible, in the midst of the City buildings, and just to the left of the Cathedral another dome can be seen, The Old Bailey. London's central criminal court, is topped with a golden statue of Justice. The Old Bailey stands on the site of the notorious Victorian prison, Newgate, and beside what was a Roman Road, we now call it 'New Oxford Street' and 'Oxford Street'. The road makes a straight track to Marble Arch and beyond. At one time this road was called The Tyburn Way, after the river which crossed it, the river which also gave its name to the gallows which stood where Marble Arch now stands.

In Victorian times on a 'hanging Day', which was known as 'Tyburn Fair', and regarded as a holiday, the unfortunates were carted from Newgate, as the bell of St. Sepulchre's tolled the knell, along that ancient road to 'Tyburn Tree', close by present day Marble Arch. On the other bank the scene is overlooked by the Royal Festival Hall and the other buildings of the South Bank, with a splendid promenade by the river. Dwarfing those buildings and just behind them is Waterloo Station with a vast new terminal which is under construction.

The River Thames widens as it flows to the east, we can see The Tower of London, Tower Bridge, and reaching skywards, Canary Wharf in Docklands. The day is especially fine and we can see almost to the North Foreland, where our flight began.

THE VIEW TO THE SOUTH

Southwards, the view is much less inspiring except that, by the River, is the magnificent 'County Hall' once the home of the Greater London Council, now largely unused, however, there are plans to turn it into a hotel. It will be a great place to stay if that happens, with its views past Westminster Bridge across the Thames and to the North.

From our aircraft we can see much further, and what a spectacular scene it is! There, by the water is the Palace of Westminster (The Houses of Parliament) with perhaps the most famous clock tower in the world 'Big Ben': the soubriquet was originally given to the great bell. The first bell was cast in Stockton on Tees and transported by sea and river to the site, however, during testing the bell cracked and was later broken and melted down. A new bell was recast in The Whitechapel Bell Foundry. This bell was nearly 14 tons in weight and it must have been a wonderful sight as a team of 16 horses pulled it on an open cart through the crowd lined streets to Westminster. During testing with a clapper which was too big, the bell cracked, however its note changed and gave it the distinctive sound with which we are familiar. In the tower it was hung with its comrades, quarter-chime bells. The chimes were arranged from the aria *'I Know That My Redeemer Liveth'* from Handel's Messiah.

And traditionally the lines:

> *All through this hour Lord be my Guide*
> *And by thy power no foot shall slide*

Accompany the chimes.

Beyond the Palace is Parliament Square, bounded on one side by Westminster Abbey and St. Margaret's church. Opposite, Whitehall stretches away to Trafalgar Square. The Banqueting House in Whitehall is the only surviving part of the old Whitehall Palace. Designed by Inigo Jones, it was completed in 1622 and stands on the site of an earlier Tudor Banqueting House. Built at the cost of £15,653/3s/3d it was faced with Portland stone and Horace Walpole described is thus:

> *'It is so complete in itself that it stands as a model of the most pure and beautiful taste'*

King Charles I commissioned the ceiling, which was painted by Rubens. The most poignant memory which the house evokes is also of Charles I. On 30th January 1649, King Charles I walked for the last time across the floor of the Banqueting House out through a window, onto the scaffold. There he was beheaded. The morning was cold, so the King wore two shirts, lest he shiver and the watching crowd think he was afraid.

GREEN LONDON

It is surprising how green London is, the greenery showing especially well from above. Opposite the Banqueting House is the Gateway to the Horse Guard's Parade, usually with mounted troopers from the Household Cavalry on guard; always a splendid sight. Through the gateway is the parade ground on which each year the Queen's birthday is celebrated with 'The Trooping Of The Colour'. We can see Buckingham Palace at the far end of St James' Park. The road on the left is known as Birdcage Walk, the walk was the site of the aviary of James I; while the road to the right is The Mall. The Mall was constructed to replace Pall Mall, as the alley for the game 'Paille Mall', a game played with a wooden mallet and a boule; 'at which game noblemen and gentlemen in France do play much'. Now The Mall with its magnificent avenue of plane trees is a 'processional way'. Buckingham Palace itself has an extensive garden, mostly hidden by a high wall from those walking up Constitution hill towards Hyde Park Corner, but it can be seen from above. To the right of Constitution Hill is Green Park bounded on its north side by Piccadilly. Things in the distance are beginning to look smaller, as from the aircraft we see Hyde Park: at the eastern end is Park Lane which finishes at Marble Arch. In the centre of Hyde

Park the Serpentine (a lake), winds its snake-like path. We can see across Kensington and the museums to the great dome of The Royal Albert Hall. Nearby, in the park, is the Albert Memorial and in the distance at the western end of the park, Kensington Palace.

As we continue our flight westwards along the river to the right is Millbank and the Tate Gallery which contains one of the finest collections of Impressionist and Post Impressionist art. Almost opposite the 'Tate' is Lambeth Palace, the official residence of the Archbishop of Canterbury. The river's course here is almost southerly, but shortly it swings to the right to flow to the west. Dominating the south bank is the immense building with four great chimneys, one at each corner, that is Battersea Power Station. Now disused, the interior has been gutted and the shell awaits an intrepid entrepreneur to find a use for, and to convert it.

Just beyond the shell of the power station is a lovely green area, Battersea Park, and on the other bank another Wren masterpiece, The Royal Hospital. The hospital was founded by King Charles II for invalid and veteran soldiers. The Chelsea Pensioners, as these veterans are now known, still wear scarlet frock coats in the summer and dark blue overcoats in winter; a uniform dating from the 18th Century.

Horse Guards Parade, St. James Park, Buckingham Palace beyond, Green Park and Hyde Park.

Left: Lambeth Palace

Below: The new MI6 HQ at Vauxhall Cross

Below: The Palace of Westminster, Big Ben and Westminster Abbey.

KEW GARDENS

The river makes an 'S' bend and narrows: there on the left, at Kew are The Royal Botanic Gardens. The gardens are of exceptional botanic interest and of historic importance. In the mid 18th Century, they originated when part of the gardens of Richmond Lodge, by Capability Brown, were taken over, to be supplemented in the next century with Kew Palace. Much of the charm of the gardens lies in the 18th century temples, greenhouses and orangery which exist amongst the rare and beautiful plants and trees.

HAMPTON COURT PALACE

The bends in the river continue as it narrows more, now it is just a stream compared with the river which could carry huge ships to London. Hampton Court Palace, with its park, nestles in one of the 'U' shaped bends in the Thames. It is probably the greatest secular building in England. The Palace has some of the most splendid architecture in the country and some buildings of great splendour by Sir Christopher Wren. Thomas Wolsey bought the site in 1514 a year before he became Cardinal and Lord Chancellor of England. He rose to those exalted positions of church and state from very

humble beginnings he was the son of an Ipswich butcher. The house was of palatial proportions with 280 rooms and a staff of about 500. Wolsey fell from grace, partly over a disagreement about Anne Boleyn: in an attempt to regain favour he gave Henry VIII Hampton Court. Wolsey did not regain his status and was eventually beheaded. Henry established Hampton Court as a Royal Palace and with its park became a favourite place with him and succeeding monarchs.

After the additions Wren completed, little has been done, and what we see today we have largely inherited from the 19th Century.

Looking ahead, the two parallel east-west runways at Heathrow can be clearly seen. Runway '28 left' is being used mainly for arrivals, while '28 right' for departures. It would be possible to land at Heathrow, but the last time I did, some years ago, the fees were over £300. There is enough fuel with reserves, so I turn and retrace the flight east, back to Southend.

Hampton Court Palace. Inset: Kew Gardens.

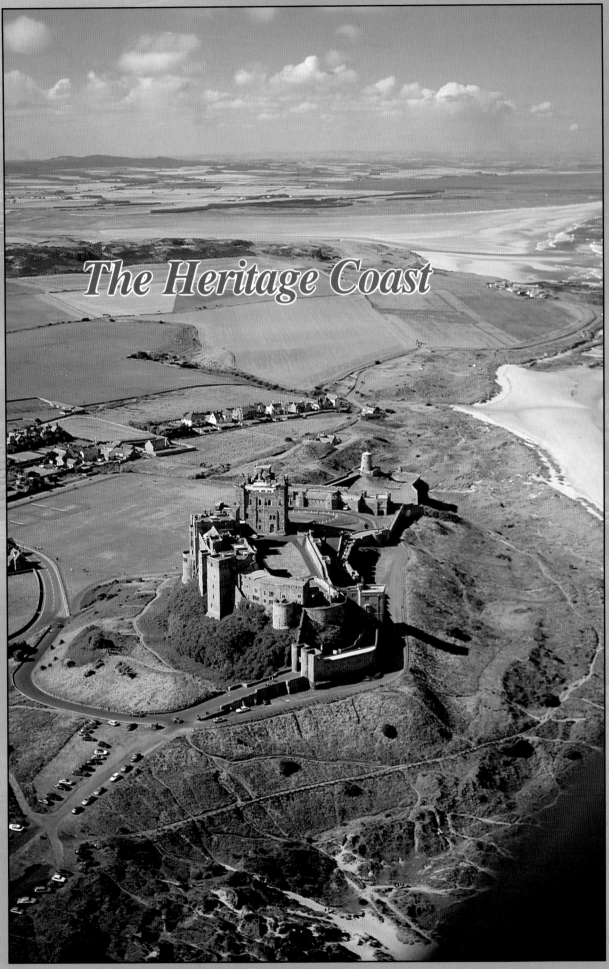

The Heritage Coast

Bamburgh Castle, looking north to Holy Island.

NORTHUMBERLAND

My first encounter with Northumberland was in 1947. The winter had been very hard, the country deep in snow. The overnight train from Kings Cross was cold but the bus from Newcastle to Hexham was warm and my companions friendly. At Hexham there was plenty of time so I set out to walk the five miles up into the hills to the sanatorium I was to visit. The brisk walk was pleasant as the lane gently rose, affording wonderful views across the snow covered fields to Hexham, a lovely town dominated by its beau-tiful minster. The hospital was comprised of bungalow buildings: the snow was so deep as to be above the roofs and I walked to the different buildings between walls of snow. My visit over, I set out on the walk back to Hexham. By now it was dark, apart from the moon which lit the snow covered scene. In the distance were the twinkling lights of the town; I paused to enjoy the view when the bells of the Abbey started to peel, calling the worshippers to evensong. So I was introduced to North-umberland and in the days I was there I explored what I could of the countryside and coast.

Seahouses

Seahouses, boarding boats for the Farne Islands

SEAHOUSES

In September 1991, I decided the time was ripe for a break, and remembering how I had enjoyed the border country before, decided to make my base Seahouses for a few days. I drove to Northumberland by way of the A1, The Great North Road. That was not too bad but once I had crossed the Tyne and was able to leave the A1 for the coast, motoring was a joy again. The narrow roads were uncluttered, there was little traffic, no traffic lights and roundabouts, and the last few miles to Seahouses, in spite of my previous long drive, left me refreshed. Bamburgh Castle Hotel stands on high ground above the harbour and commands fine views of the fishing and pleasure boats as they depart and return. Beyond the harbour lie the delightful Farne Islands.

The Farne Islands

THE FARNE ISLANDS

Along this unspoilt stretch of coast, the Farne Islands are noted for the vast colonies of sea birds and as the home of the grey seal. The islands were known as Farena Ealande in Anglo Saxon times (considered to be from the departure of the Romans in the 5th century until the Norman conquest in 1066, sometimes called the Dark Ages although recent thought is tending to change that opinion.)

The name Farne is probably derived from that Anglo Saxon name meaning 'Island of Pilgrims'. When weather conditions and tides permit, it is easy to take a boat trip from Seahouses Harbour around the Farnes to enjoy seeing the seals basking on the rocks and diving in the sea: nearby a myriad of sea birds cover the islands they have made their home. Visitors are allowed to land on Staple Island, and the paths and hides which have been constructed make it easy to come close to the birds.

There are some twenty eight islands in the Farne group.

They are part of the Great Whin Sill, a geological feature which extends from the islands, inland. The great castle at Bamburgh and the ruined castle at Dunstanburgh are built on its crags and much further away near Hexham the Romans took advantage of this natural majestic ridge and built Hadrian's wall along its summit.

Situated and scattered as they are just a few miles from the coast, the Farne Islands have been a hazard to shipping for centuries, and it is believed that the monks who lived their simple monastic life on the islands kept beacons burning to warn seafarers of the treacherous rocks; many of which are underwater for much of the time. In 1500 Prior Castell's Tower was constructed on the Inner Farne to contain the beacon, and later Charles II granted a licence for the first official lighthouse. This beacon fire was lit each evening at the top of Prior Castell's Tower. Even so, wrecks continued and in the mid18th century Trinity House constructed the first real lighthouse.

The Farnes, Staple Island.

GRACE DARLING

On the 5th September, 1838, The Forfarshire set sail from Hull bound for Dundee with a cargo of cloth, hardware, soap and with a complement of twenty four crew and thirty nine passengers. It was a stormy night as the ship approached the Farnes and the captain chose the more sheltered route between the islands and the mainland. Late that night Captain Humble mistook the Longstone Light for the Inner Farne and drove the 400 ton vessel onto the rocks. Grace lived on the Longstone light with her parents: her father William Darling was the keeper of the light. Looking from her window in the early hours of the 7th of September, Grace saw the wreck of the Forfarshire. Legend has it that she heard the cries of the survivors. Grace and her father launched a rowing boat. a Northumbrian 'coble' and made two journeys to the wreck and rescued eight men and a woman.

Much publicity followed and Grace Darling became the epitome of a Victorian heroine. She received a gift from Queen Victoria and others from public subscription, she had many proposals of marriage and made several lecture tours. Grace did marry, but sadly died at the early age of 27.

'The Grace Darling', coble used in rescue

The 'coble' used in the rescue can be seen together with much memorabilia of the period in the Grace Darling Museum in the village of Bamburgh. Grace rests in an ornate grave overlooking the sea and the Farne Islands in the churchyard at Bamburgh. The church is mainly 13th century and is dedicated to the Lindisfarne's Saint Aidan. During restoration in 1837, a most unusual 13th century crypt was discovered with coffins of the Foster Family who once owned Bamburgh; but it is thought the crypt was built to hold relics of St. Aidan.

Church of St. Aidan, Grace Darling Tomb

A FLIGHT ALONG THE HERITAGE COAST

At first, after fruitless telephone calls to various aerodromes I thought that a flight was going to be impossible. The staff in the hotel knew I was looking for an aircraft and the chef sought me out saying,

"I hear you are looking for a flight in a light aircraft," to which I replied, "Yes, but I have had no luck in finding one."

"A farmer I know has his own aircraft, perhaps he can help. Here is his phone number," he said.

A couple of phone calls later I had located Peter Bell. Peter operated a transport company called 'Bells Fargo' and a 'Citabria' two place aircraft from his own landing strip on a disused WWII aerodrome just to the south of Morpeth. The day was perfect for both flying and air photography, the wind was light, I could see 'forever' and the sky was 'dusted' with fair weather cumulus; a cloud which must have been designed to enhance photographs.

"When can we fly?" I asked Peter.

"How about now?" he replied.

So I set off for his 'aerodrome' and met Peter busy refuelling the 'Citabria' for our flight. I climbed aboard the little aircraft, it had tandem seating; I sat behind the pilot and before the engines were started, checked that the windows would open fully, I do not 'shoot' through perspex. The windows opened out and up, affording a clear unobstructed view; perfect! Peter pressed the starter, the engine burst into life and we moved off to the 'holding point', a designated place just before the runway where the pilot completes his final checks before take off, we call them 'vital actions.' Soon we are accelerating down the runway for our peaceful photographic sortie from an aerodrome from which hundreds of R.A.F. Lancasters trundled, nearly fifty years ago on more sinister intent.

As we became airborne the land and skyscape opened up and the visibility was unlimited. The sky was dappled with 'fair weather cumulus' and as we climbed the horizon retreated all around until at two thousand feet we could see about fifty miles in each direction. We turned north east towards Holy Island as we were going to fly there then turn south to follow this wonderful coastline of low lying sand dunes and long, wide, lonely beaches.

Peter Bell with his Citabria aircraft

HOLY ISLAND AND LINDISFARNE

In 634, Oswald, King of Northumbria and a Christian convert, from his capital Bebbanburgh (Bamburgh) sent to the Christian Community at Iona for a missionary. First came Corman; but he found the Northumbrians 'uncivilised, obstinate and barbarous', so he returned to Iona. Then a year later Aidan arrived in Northumbria. Aidan chose the Island site which we now call Holy Island, close to the royal residence at Bebbenburgh, to set up his ministry.

Holy Island is connected to the mainland by a causeway which is only passable at low tide: between the island and mainland is a natural harbour with excellent shelter for small boats. On this lonely desolate place Aidan built his church and monastery. Aidan's ministry flourished and the gentle Anglo Saxon creed coupled with a love of nature, spread in all directions including Holland. A school was established and four of the children who came to be educated were brothers, Cedd, Cynebil, Caelin and Chad all became priests while Chad and Cedd were later ordained bishops.

In the early 7th century, Sebert the Saxon King of what we now call Essex, had embraced the Christian faith. Sebert wishing his subjects to be converted also, sent to Aidan at Lindisfarne for a missionary; Cedd was chosen. He, together with a few companions, boarded a little boat in the harbour behind Holy Island. From there they set off on their treacherous voyage down the North Sea, to land at the wharf of the abandoned Roman Fort, Othona, on the Essex coast at Bradwell in 654. There Cedd established his community, and built his chapel astride the wall of the fort. This simple little building still stands today: it is still consecrated and used for worship. It is known as St. Peter's on the Wall. Saxon King Sebert rests in the ancient churchyard of Great Burstead just by a venerable yew, perhaps as old as the king, but still flourishing.

The monks left Lindisfarne in 875, and it seems likely the Island was abandoned until a cell of Benedictine monks were granted the See of Lindisfarne. They renamed the island 'Holy Island' and rebuilt the priory, dedicating it to St Cuthbert (the 6th bishop of Lindisfarne 685-687). Peace reigned for about 450 years until it was destroyed in the dissolution. The present ruins retain a peace and serenity imparted by that holy man Aidan and his Saintly followers, and these remnants, together with the beautiful 'Rainbow Arch', are an impressive testimony to bygone elegance.

There is a castle built on a great outcrop of rock on the island. It was started by King Henry VIII with materials from the vandalised Priory and was known as the 'Fort of Beblowe' (Beblowe being the ancient name of the outcrop or hill on which it is built).

But perhaps it is the Lindisfarne Gospels which are the finest heritage we have remaining from those times when the monks of Aidan's Community were spreading the Gospel through the land. They are probably the finest surviving example of Celtic Art. They were created by Eadfrith (Bishop of Lindisfarne 698-721) in honour of Saint Cuthbert. The Gospels were taken from Lindisfarne with other relics when the monks fled the Island in 875. Thereafter some legends prevail but there is no record of what happened to this unique work until they miraculously reappeared in the seventeenth century. They can be seen today in the British Museum.

Lindisfarne. Inset: Effigy of St. Aidan

Lindisfarne Abbey

The Fort of Beblow, Holy Island.

BAMBURGH

Peter turned the 'Citabria' south and on that brilliant day we could see the great arms of the breakwaters at Newcastle which marks the entrance to the River Tyne, some forty nautical miles away. Much closer, just off-shore the sea was dotted with the Farne Islands and abeam, close by the beach, standing grand on a promontory was Bamburgh Castle, surely one of the grandest castles in England.

Taking advantage of the massive basalt crag, which is part of the geological feature known as the Great Whin Sill the Saxon King Ida built a wooden fortification there. It was given by his grandson Ethelfrith to his wife Bebba and became known as Bebbanburgh, from which the modern name derives. Bamburgh remained a royal residence until Norman times when it was rebuilt, a great stone keep added, curtain walls and chapel built, together with all the ancillary buildings to complete a wondrous Norman Castle. It was last besieged in 1464 and was used by Henry VI as his capital during the Wars of the Roses. Standing as it does on a rocky precipice which rises 150 feet from the beach, Bamburgh dominates the view from the sea. Although the hill is sheer towards the sea, the other side of the crag slopes more gently down to the village of the same name. In recent times the castle has been beautifully restored and looks majestic against the golden sands and blue sea by day and the dark starry sky when floodlit at night.

Bamburgh Castle and the Farne Islands

We flew towards the Farne Islands, but not too close, so as not to disturb the wildlife. Bamburgh Castle was a magnificent sight from our vantage point about a thousand feet above. The North sea was brilliant blue, the wide lonely sands, golden, edged with lines of gentle white waves born of the light wind.

Just behind the castle which dominated the scene is the village of Bamburgh with the 13th century church of St. Aidan close by the sea with the Victorian tomb of Grace Darling far the largest monument in the churchyard. There are expansive views beyond Bamburgh across miles of farmland until, in the distance, the beautiful Cheviots, dappled with sunlight and shadows from the clouds above, rise to fill the sky.

The great main gate, atop a gentle rise, with towers on each side and walls protecting each side of the entrance up to the main castle walls, is at the southern end.

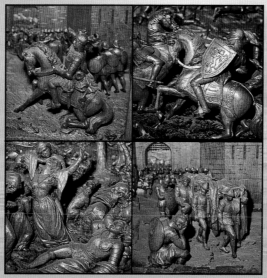
Carvings from the Chevy Chase Sideboard

This is border country and very often the warriors north of the border would make a foray south, and just as often the gates of Bamburgh would swing open and a raiding party would pour out and sally north. It is strange how coincidence weaves its patterns. I was staying in an 18th Century coaching inn, The Grosvenor in Shaftsbury, Dorset when, walking through a corridor, I noticed a sign, The Chevy Chase Room; being of a curious nature I went in. There at the end of the room was a magnificent carved wooden sideboard depicting the Battle of Otterburn which inspired the ballad of the Chevy Chase. Created between 1857 and 1863, the sideboard has carvings which depict the warriors leaving Bamburgh Castle, The Battle of Otterburn and later the dead, including Lord Percy borne home by his comrades in arms to the gates of Bamburgh Castle.

The battle was rather more than a skirmish. The ancient Ballad of 'Chevy Chase' is too long to reproduce here, but these few stanzas will give an idea of the ferocity of the moonlight battle:

From the Ballad of Chevy Chase

Then the Percy out of Banborowe Came, (Bamburgh)
  With him a mighty meinye, (Company)
With fifteen hundred archers bold
  Chosen out of shirès three.

The doughty Douglas on a steed
  Rode all his men beforn;
His armour glitter'd as did a gleed, (live coal)
  Bolder bairne was never born. (Fighting man)

With that an arrow came hastily
  Forth of a mighty wane; (host or multitude)
And it hath striken the Earl Douglas
  In at the breastè-bane

(All this there saw) a Scottish knight,
  Sir Hugh of Montgomerye:
When he saw Douglas to the death was dight, (doomed)
  Through a hundred archerye
He never stint nor he never blint (stint-stay/blint-stopped)
  Till he came on Lord Percye.

He set upon the Lord Percy
  A dint that was full sore; (dint-lunge)
With a surè spear of a mighty tree
  Thro' the body him he bore,
O' the t'other side that man might see
  A large cloth-yard and more.

Of fifteen hundred archers of England
  Went away but seventy-and-three;
Of twenty hundred spearmen of Scotland
  But even five-and-fifty

There was slain with the bold Percye
  Sir John of Agerstoune,
Sir Roger, the hendè Hartley,
  Sir William, the bold Herone.

Jesu Christ! our balès bete, (balès-woes)
  And to the bliss us bring! (bete-better,relieve)
This was the hunting of the Cheviot:
  God send us all good ending.

It is said that the Scots were the victors of the battle of Chevy Chase (Otterburn) if a victor could be defined from such carnage.

DUNSTANBURGH CASTLE

Here on another outcrop of the Great Whin Sill stands the eerie skeleton of a great castle. Rearing on a basalt crag more than 100 feet above the sea, little remains of the mighty Norman castle, but there are some remnants of the curtain wall, of a tower and gatehouse. Turner found romantic inspiration in these ruins, set as they are against sea and sky, and he painted the scene thrice.

Little coloured quartz stones are found in cracks on the crag; they are known as Dunstanburgh Diamonds. While on the shore, a cavern into which waves rush, rolling the stones and sending up sprays of water with a great noise, is known as the "Rumbling Churn".

Dunstanburgh Castle looking north. **Top:** *Bamburgh Castle, floodlit at night.*

ALNWICK

We flew a few more miles south to the charming seaside village of Alnmouth, now a tiny holiday resort, but once an important grain-shipping port and even a smugglers' haven. Alnmouth was the port for Alnwick, exporting corn and importing timber. Then on Christmas Day in 1806, a great storm changed the course of the Aln so that the river poured into the sea on the north side of the village. The harbour to the south was abandoned and gradually silted up.

Church Hill was the site of an Anglo Saxon church, which was probably the meeting place of the Great Synod of 684 in which Cuthbert was chosen Bishop of Lindisfarne. The later Norman church which replaced the Anglo Saxon building, was finally destroyed in the great storm. Occasionally the little town was bombarded from the sea once in 1799 when the American John Paul Jones (see The Captain and The Candlestick, *Above the Lakes*) fired a 68lb. cannonball at the church; it missed, bounced three times and crashed into a farmhouse.

Following the river Aln inland, we soon came to Alnwick. Alnwick, a convenient resting place, about halfway between Newcastle on Tyne and Berwick on Tweed, grew up on the River Aln beside the great border castle. Now the town betrays its age in narrow cobbled streets, passages, gateways and grey stone buildings. Around the castle are grounds landscaped by Capability

Brown in 1765 which form a beautiful riverside park. A barbican, (outwork of a fortified place, especially to defend a drawbridge) topped with figures, guards the gateway to Alnwick Castle. The castle was started in the 12th century by the de Vesci family and has been added to and restored a number of times since, although what we see from above is largely unchanged since the 14th century. With great walls, a huge keep with flanking towers, the massive castle is a superb example of a medieval fortress yet still it is a ducal residence. For many years it has been, and still is, the home of the Earls and Dukes of Northumberland.

Alnmouth

Left: Alnwick Castle

Alnwick

WARKWORTH

Not far from the coastal dunes and the sea, the River Coquet bends in a perfect horseshoe shape, and nestling in this bend is the charming village of Warkworth: the open end of the 'horseshoe' is closed with the majestic ruins of the castle, very reminiscent of a 'Motte-and-

into the hills and the river led us to Rothbury. Yes!- sometimes we pilots follow rivers and roads instead of radio beacons; when the weather is right it is far more interesting. Rothbury has a history which dates back well before the Norman Conquest. Set as it is in the Cheviot Hills it is an ideal centre for touring: for us circling above there were expansive wonderful views in

Warkworth

Bailey' castle. The unusually-shaped keep at Warkworth stands on a mound while the curtain wall surrounds the bailey. I stayed once at the Sun Hotel in Warkworth, set beside the winding river and in the shadow of the castle. It was springtime and the grassy banks down to the water and up to the walls of the castle were covered with daffodils.

TO HEXHAM

We reluctantly turned our tail on the sea and the coast and followed the River Coquet into the Cheviots. The day was remaining very beautiful; sometimes as the sun gets higher and stronger, more clouds bubble up until the sky is completely covered and there is very little light below. Today, only about half the sky is covered (in aviation it is described as '4 octas' that is 4 eighths of the sky covered) which is perfect for photography; a blank sky makes for bland pictures. Soon we gently climbed

each direction. The River Cocquet meandered its way to the west, while wide expanses of forest covered the high ground to the north and south, and there about 25 miles away was the valley of the River Tyne.

To the west we could see the sea we had not long since left; but much closer, just outside Rothbury is Cragside. Here surrounding 'Nelly's Moss Lakes is a Country Park of unequalled beauty. Meadows give way to forests, forests slope down to lakes and in the midst of it all, a magnificent house; Cragside. Gardens surround the house and its Pinetum Gorge has a gentle path down to the valley and River Coquet. However, perhaps the most interesting feature is the Power Circuit, a two mile circular walk which takes you to all the original machinery created by Lord Armstrong to provide electric power to the house, the first to have hydro-electric power.

We now turned south crossed Otterburn and looked down on the site of that terrible battle and a short while later came to Hexham.

Cragside and Country Park. Inset: Cragside, the first house to to be lit by hydro-electricity.

HEXHAM

Peter throttled back, reduced speed and took some flap; the aircraft was now in its 'slow safe configuration'. We could now gently circle the town and as I looked down on the Minster, memories of that day in 1947 came flooding back. Then it was winter, and the fields were snow covered, now it is spring with the trees and flowers bursting into life, then it was dark and I could not see Hexham. Now, in brilliant afternoon sunlight, the town, set by the River Tyne, is spread out below. In the centre, beside the market square stands the 12th century Minster, its square tower housing the ancient bells I had heard peal all those years ago. Today the only sound was the steady and comforting drone of the engine; in 1947 as I walked those silent country lanes the sound of the Minster's bells drifted across the countryside as they called the congregation to evensong.

Stone for the first church came from the Roman Fort called Corstopitum; the church which was dedicated to

St. Andrew was completed in 678; said, for its day, to have been a magnificent building. Now all that remains of that first building is the crypt, the finest Anglo Saxon crypt in England. In the crypt some of the stones with inscriptions betray their Roman origins. The mellow stone of St. Andrews looked especially attractive touched as it was by the lowering afternoon sun.

Situated as it is about half way between Newcastle and the North Sea to the east and Carlisle and the Irish Sea to

Hexham Minster

the west, the beautiful town of Hexham is an ideal base to explore the surrounding countryside; notably Hadrian's Wall and Housesteads Roman Fort.

HADRIAN'S WALL

Just to the south of Hexham the Romans took advantage of the natural escarpment the Great Whin Sill and built their wall on its summit, taking advantage of the sheer drop on the northern side and the gentle slope to the south. Here too is the great fort, Housesteads, one of the garrisons which served the 'wall'. The first reference to be found in ancient literature is, "Hadrian was the first to build a wall, 80 miles long, to separate the Romans from the Barbarians." The undertaking was tremendous, for it was not just a wall which was constructed but a defensive system.

In 118AD there was a rebellion and Hadrian's biographer quotes, "Britons could no longer be held under control." The rebellion was put down and in 122AD the Emperor Hadrian came to Britain. In the absence of a natural barrier it was decreed that a wall should be built to define the northern extent of the Roman Empire and also provide protection from the northern barbarians. So a wall was constructed eventually, from Wallsend on Tyne in the east, to Bowness on the Solway Firth in the west. The wall was 80 Roman miles long, (a Roman mile is 1620 yards) much of it built with stone. Small forts, large enough for a complement of about fifty men, were constructed every Roman Mile, they are now known as milecastles. Every third of a mile had a turret or look out

The Great Whinsill and Hadrian's Wall. Housesteads can be seen in the mid distance.

post, so that each milecastle had a turret on each side. The main stone wall was some 10 feet thick and 15 foot high to the rampart walk; the western section of the wall where limestone for mortar was not so freely available was constructed of turf. In front of the wall for its length was a 'V' shaped ditch and behind the wall, first a military way for quick deployment of troops, and behind that a double bank and ditch complex, known as the Vallum. This mainly marked the southern boundary of the military zone, a zone forbidden to civilians. This whole complex was backed with great forts: there were 17 in all; some could accommodate 1000 cavalry. There were also supply depots, like the one at Corbridge. A full complement of troops for the wall was something like thirty-five thousand men in its heyday, and the Romans garrisoned it for about two hundred and fifty years. That was Hadrian's Wall. Then we were flying above the section which follows the Whin Sill: below was the finest of the forts left to us, Housesteads (Roman Vercovicium). These fascinating remains contain the only Roman Hospital to be found in Britain and a latrine with a flushing tank. The day was still beautiful with the cumulus clouds producing shadows: photographic subjects like Housesteads

look dull in the shadow so we had to circle for a while waiting for the fort to be bathed in sunshine. There were breathtaking views across the Northumbrian National Park to the north and of a large sections of the wall both east and west.

The magnificence of this scene on such a beautiful day should not deceive us about life for the soldiers in those far off days. In winter, a northerly wind would be driving freezing rain, drenching the sentries, chilling them to the bone as they wearily trudged the ramparts. They would curse the lurking foe and think soldiers thoughts of warmer climes, of home and friends. Meanwhile there were a few gaming houses and brothels huddled in the lee of the wall to bring some relief from the weather and boredom. Reluctantly we had to leave this fascinating scene and turn west to follow the line of the wall to the Solway. There was not too much of the wall to see to the west. Soon Carlisle came into view; just north of the city meandered the River Eden. Hadrian's Wall followed this river fairly closely and so did we, until we came to Bowness, the end of the Roman wall and the end of our flight of exploration. From there we landed at Carlisle to refuel before returning to base.

Housesteads Fort. I had to circle awaiting the sun to come onto the fort.

Here at Solway Firth we end our
Heritage Flight and begin to fly...

Above the Lakes
and
between the Peaks

With poems from
'How the Lake District was Made'
and 'Lake District Yellow Bonnets'
by Aileen Otley

Solway Firth

BEGINNINGS

It is said that a country without history is a happy country. The lake district has very little history and is now a very beautiful, tranquil place. Unlike Cumbria's neighbour, Northumberland, the mountains, lakes and narrow treacherous passes did not lend themselves to war and so the turmoil of conflict largely left Cumbria alone.

There was at one time great turmoil for, at the same time the Thames Valley was being formed; massive volcanic forces threw up great rocks which we now call, Scafell, Skiddaw and Helvellyn to name a few, between their steep sides, rivers ran, hollows became lakes and in time erosion, trees and vegetation mellowed the landscape and great prehistoric creatures ruled the land.

In the mean time it is ours to explore and enjoy. There are valleys and passes to wander through, mountains to climb, fells to walk and flower-edged lakes to rest by. I have travelled much in the Alps, they are vast and wonderful, yet I found the Lakes of Cumbria more enchanting in a way.

It is possible that the smaller scale of our Lake District produces ever-changing vistas. Lush valleys change to boulder-strewn passes, gently undulating country becomes dominated with snow capped peaks, a towering waterfall changes to a stream, the stream becomes a lake of calm waters reflecting the tree clad hills around. It is no wonder that the 19th century poets found their inspiration amongst all this magnificence.

The Prehistoric Creatures went away
But will come back another day.

THE LAKE DISTRICT belongs to Them, you see,
They only LEND it to YOU and ME!

Aileen Otley.

Little Langdale.

Grasmere

GRASMERE

It was here in what is the centre of the Lake District, that William Wordsworth, the most famed of the Lake Poets, made his home in Dove Cottage. The cottage was built as an inn in the early 17th century and for the next 170 years was known as the 'Dove and Olive'. On a bitterly cold December day in 1799, William and his sister Dorothy moved in. The empty cottage was soon made into a comfortable home, in those days it overlooked the fields to Grasmere Village and the parish church of St. Oswald. Behind the cottage they created a garden which you can walk in today. William married, children came, the cottage had an ever open-door for their friends. The small house must have been a bustling yet happy place. The evenings were spent around the fire, the light from which was supplemented with combined candle and rushlight. Wordsworth described the lights of Hawkshead:

> And in the frosty season, when the sun
> Was set, and visible for many a mile
> The cottage windows through the twilight blazed.
>
> From The Prelude.

Surely Dove Cottage must have looked like that, and-

> In the loved presence of the cottage-fire
> And listen to the flapping of the flame
> Or kettle whispering its faint undersong.
>
> From Personal Talk.

By 1808 William his family and friends had outgrown Dove Cottage and I am sure the day was tinged with

sadness as they moved away to nearby Rydal Mount.

Now Dove Cottage is very much as it was and a visit is a fascinating experience. Nearby is a superb museum administered by The Wordsworth Trust.

William Wordsworth moved back to Grasmere on his death in 1850, now he rests in the churchyard of St. Oswald, beside the River Rothay in company with Dorothy his sister, his beloved daughter Dora and other members of his family.

St Oswald's Church. Painting by Ron Slade

Dove Cottage, Grasmere. Inset: Candlestick and rushlight used in Dove Cottage. Painting by Ron Slade.

ABOVE THE LAKES AND MOUNTAINS

Hadrian's Wall begins in the East at Wallsend on Tyne, spans the country, comes close to Carlisle for a while, follows the River Eden and ends on the Solway Firth by Bowness-on-Solway. It was the Roman way of saying, "Beyond here is Roman rule." The country is also flat for some miles before the dramatically rising ground of the 'Lake District'.   Carlisle Airport is on the flat ground a little to the north east of the city. Once a wartime base, now its activity is much reduced and like many an airfield is rich in wildlife. Hares were at play, Lapwings and seabirds were everywhere the air was filled with the plaintive call of curlews. There I met Bill Dixon.

direction 220 degrees from north). As the throttle was opened, 'Bravo Foxtrot' accelerated, 20,30,40,50 knots: at 55 Bill moved the control column gently back, we were airborne a slight left turn and there ahead rising out of the plain was the Lake District.

Carlisle Airport. Top: Bill Dixon and his 'Cessna 152'.

When I have a question time after a slide presentation the most frequent question I am asked is, "How do you fly the aircraft and take pictures at the same time?" The simple answer is, "I don't, I always take another pilot to do the flying." Today it was to be Bill who lives locally and knows the lakes well, leaving me to concentrate on the photography.

Our aircraft was a high wing 'Cessna 152, 'Bravo Foxtrot'. Bill completed the preflight checks, the aircraft was O.K., and lined up on runway '22' (That is with a

Just to the left of the aircraft's nose, the great cone that is Skiddaw stood sentinel, filling the sky. To the right was the steeply rising ground that is Wythop, Broom Fell, Lord's Seat, and Ladies Table, a vast flat rock which was a favourite picnic place of the Victorians, now almost hidden in the trees and forgotten. Extending from the plain between Skiddaw and Wythop, lies Bassenthwaite Lake and beyond the lake, in the far distance, still snow covered, Langdale Pikes.

Bassenthwaite, Skiddaw and Langdale Pikes

As we flew along The Wythop Valley, below, the still waters of Bassenthwaite Lake reflected the dense forests rising from the shoreline and extending up the hills on each side. The question is sometimes asked. "How many lakes are there in the Lake District?" The answer is, one, Bassenthwaite: all the others are meres, waters or tarns. The southern end of the lake gave way to a beautiful area of woodlands and meadows through which runs the River Derwent connecting with Derwentwater: this is The Vale of Keswick with the lovely town of Keswick nestling close by the water's edge. Soon, down below, was Castlerigg Fell and clearly in view from our privileged position, on an open site, was a ring of great boulders, The Castlerigg Stone Circle.

The Castlerigg Stones are contemporary with Stonehenge and were created by Bronze age man some 4500-5000 years ago yet in Wordsworth's time they were thought to be associated with the Druid cult, an opinion which persisted until recent times.

The ancient Castlerigg Stone Circle.

> *"...The primal truth Glimmers through many a superstitious form."*

William Wordsworth, (Ecclesiastical Sonnet)

Derwentwater, Keswick, Skiddaw and Saddleback

By now fair weather cumulus were scattered across the sky, we were now flying at 3500 feet. To the east in the distance was Thirlmere, a long narrow stretch of water. Below was a scattering of cloud, while beyond Thirlmere the steeply rising ground which is Helvellyn was capped by the last of the winter snow, which in turn was topped by a layer of cloud which had been lifted by the hills. "This scene of unsurpassed beauty alone makes all the work and training worthwhile," remarked Bill.

which it is connected by a loop of road and is dominated by St. Oswald's church.

Not raised in nice proportions was the Pile
But large and massy, for duration built,
With pillars crowded and the roof upheld
By naked rafters intricately crossed.

William Wordsworth.

Yellow Bonnets

Yellow Bonnets, the daffodils,
at the end of the lonning

Suprised, are you
the world is still here
as you re-appear from earth
and grace the green

As I walk past you I shall stop
then turn and see you more closely
and then hear you whispering
See your nodding Yellow Bonnets
Like congregation
Nodding
leaving wooden pew.

Aileen Otley

From 'Lake District Yellow Bonnets'

Dora's Field, Rydale. Painting by Ron Slade.

Soon we were in the Heart of Lakeland: below were the 'twin' small lakes, Rydal and Grasmere. Here William Wordsworth lived, died and now rests beside the River Rothay which flows on into Grasmere there in the centre of the lake is the tree covered island to which Wordsworth his family and friends would often row, to picnic and enjoy each others company in that innermost sanctuary amidst the hills. The Rothay emerges at the other end of Grasmere to meander the half mile through meadows and woods and on into Rydal water beside which, on the hillside, is Rydal Mount. The grounds especially remain very much as Wordsworth left them when he died in 1850. To the south of both lakes the ground rises steeply to the straggling heights of Loughrigg Fell, while to the north is broad valley and the charming village of Grasmere, just off the main road to

Reluctantly we turned the aircraft north: it was time to return. We flew back past Thirlmere on to Derwent Water and Keswick and there ahead was the majestic heights of The Saddleback and Skiddaw. "How is the fuel?" I asked Bill

"Enough for an hour and a half," he replied and Carlisle Airport is only fifteen minutes away.

"Then let us do a turn round Skiddaw," I said.

And so we did: sometimes below the level of the summit, we looked down on the sharp crown and steep sides of the Saddleback of Bencathra, into the water-filled hollow which is Scales Tarn and volcanic evidence of the tumultuous long ago creation of this beautiful place. Reluctantly we turned the aircraft's tail on Skiddaw and flew back to Carlisle. It was a truly memorable flight.

Thirlmere and Helvellyn

*What was the great Parnassus' self' to thee
Mount Skiddaw? In his natural sovereignty
Our British hill is fairer far; he shrouds
His double front among Atlantic clouds,
And pours forth streams more sweet than Castally.*

—*William Wordsworth.*

Saddleback, Scales Tarn and Skiddaw

AGAIN-INTO THE MOUNTAINS

Sometimes when pilots fly together they practice emergency procedures. On this flight I decided to give Bill a practice engine failure. No danger was involved, I would just close the throttle, the engine would still idle; then Bill would choose a field, go through the 'emergency drills' and position the aircraft towards the field, then at 500ft. above the ground, the practice complete, we would climb away.

As we headed towards the coast I was looking for a suitable area, it needs to be where people or animals would not be worried. The day was gorgeous, the wind was light, the visibility superb and the sky dotted again with fair weather cumulus, but when I looked at the fields 2500ft. below they were peppered with white dots, some large with two smaller satellites orbiting nearby; they were sheep with their lambs, I have never seen so many. Our practice forced landing was impossible.

WHITEHAVEN

We reached the coast to see a gentle Irish Sea lapping the shoreline near Whitehaven. The day was beautiful and the visibility almost unlimited; we flew a mile or two out to sea and the view was splendid. There was the compact town of Whitehaven with the breakwaters of its harbour reaching out into the sea. Beyond the town a few miles of flat ground gave way to the mountains of lakeland. South along the coast we could see the vast nuclear complex which is Sellafield. The town has its roots in coal-mining and The Old Quay in Whitehaven Harbour has some of the oldest coaling wharfs in Britain. Work on The Old Quay was begun in 1634 and the wharfs were constructed to ship the locally mined coal to the towns in the south. The town, which was developed by the Lowther family around the harbour in the 17th and 18th centuries, has great charm and a number of elegant old houses survive today. The harbour is now used to receive phosphate

Above: Whitehaven.

Left: Factory discharging effluent into the Irish Sea.

from North Africa for the works on the cliff above the sea where they are turned into detergents. Close by the harbour is a building which is reminiscent of a Norman Castle, however it is a coal mine.

The mine was modernised in the 1840's and massive stone walls in medieval style were built around the mine shaft, yet even more interesting is the candlestick shaped ventilation shaft.

THE CAPTAIN AND THE CANDLESTICK

One of the most interesting characters to hail from Whitehaven was John Paul, a sea captain. After he ran a mutineer through with his sword he decided not to risk a trial and fled Whitehaven for America. There he was given command of 'Ranger' one of the first ships commissioned for the American Navy during the War of Independence. Later, this led him to be called "The Founder of the American Navy."

As a 'cover up' John Paul added Jones to his name and this colourful personality became, John Paul Jones.

He sailed for the Solway and, knowing Whitehaven well, he returned with his ship, attacked shipping in the harbour and raided the town. However, a renegade from his crew alerted the townsfolk who rushed down to the harbour and the raiders took to their boats and fled back to their ship. Interestingly this was the last time an enemy power was to land on the English mainland.

Popular legend has it that some of the invaders descended on Lowther Castle and stole a considerable amount of silver. Amongst the plunder was a candlestick, a present to Lord Lowther from the King of Prussia to mark the King's visit to Whitehaven. The candlestick was of great sentimental value to the Lowther family, and a reward was offered for its return. John Paul Jones heard of this, a truce was arranged. The Captain returned to Whitehaven and together with his escort paraded the candlestick from the harbour down the main street of Whitehaven back to Lowther castle. Lord Lowther was so pleased at the return of the candlestick that when the mine was rebuilt the ventilation shaft was created in the form of a candlestick in commemoration of the event.

FROM WHITEHAVEN

From Whitehaven looking south, and not too far away on a cliff-top, the detergent factory is still discharging its effluent into the Irish Sea. The day is superb, and about 20 miles further south, beyond St. Bees Head, on the plain where the mountains move closer to the sea the steam from the cooling towers at the Sellafield nuclear plant can be clearly seen. As we neared Sellafield we had to move a few miles out to sea to avoid the danger area which surrounds the plant.

Yet even so the site was impressive: in the centre is the vast new building which I am told is large enough to house the ocean liner Queen Elizabeth II. South, beyond the danger area, we were able to turn towards the mountains again and there ahead was Wasdale and Wast

Water, a lake which almost fills the valley. It is the deepest of the lakes; and it is easy to see why. From the southern shore the ground continues to rise steeply to almost 2000 feet and part of the surface is covered with screes (steep slopes covered with loose fragments of rock) Although on the opposite side the rise is less steep, the forest covered slope continues to nearly 2300 feet. The valley is open at the seaward end but at the far end, still snow-capped is Scarfell Pike, the highest peak in England at 3162 feet: but even that was capped, like the icing on a cake by a layer of cumulous cloud. What a magnificent view!

HARD KNOTT PASS

Said to be the most difficult pass in the lake district with hairpin bends and gradients of 1:3 driving this route even when conditions are good is difficult, yet here we were effortlessly enjoying a view of the pass from a little below the peaks which surround it. Hard Knott joins with the Wrynose Pass and together they complete the route

Sellafield

from Ambleside, Roman Galava to the coast and port of Ravenglass Roman Glannaventa. This route from their port to the more gentle inland area must have been important in Roman times so they built a fort on the high ground looking over the Eskdale Valley to the sea and Glannaventa guarding the narrow end of the Hard Knott pass.

It must have been a desolate posting for the soldiers, yet even so, they had a little Roman Luxury: they installed a bathhouse.

Hard Knott Pass

Wastwater with Screes

BACK TO CARLISLE

Beyond the eastern end of Hard Knott, in the distance, snow covered, The Langdale Pikes disappeared into the cloud. It would not have been safe to fly following the valleys below the cloud, so we climbed to 5000 feet turned north and set course for the airfield. Our route took us across Langdale, towards Ullswater where through a break in the cloud we saw the tree-covered slopes of Gowborrow Park and had a glimpse of Aira Force, lakelands best known waterfall.

When the last Deinosuchus wept, of course,
His tears made Aira Force!
And if you can climb a path on a hill,
Aira Force is cascading still.

Aileen Otley

Above: Langdale Pikes

Right: Aira Force

FAREWELL CUMBRIA, THE PEAKS
AND THE LAKES

The high ground of the Lake District faces the west from where most of our clouds come. So, as the mild warm air reaches the mountains, it is lifted by the high ground, the moisture is squeezed from the air and falls as rain making lakeland the wettest place in England. It was Good Friday when, quite early in the morning I met Bill once more at Carlisle Airport. We were going to have one more flight into the mountains and as we climbed out from the airport threatening clouds were filling the sky from the west. Our farewell flight was short, we flew once more around Skiddaw then returned to base. Bill and I gained much from flying together, he from my experience as a flying instructor and me from Bill's knowledge of the Lake District.

The nature of flying is that, 'it is a very small world'

so I am sure that the time will come when I will walk into some distant airport and hear a cry, "Hi Edward, remember me!" Then Bill and I will reminisce again about the time and flying we enjoyed together 'Above the Lakes and between the Peaks' way back in ninety-three.

I pointed my car south from Carlisle and started my journey, first for a drive through the lakes, then back to Essex.

The mountains had been busy, lifting the moist air and filling the clouds with rain which fell as a deluge onto the hillsides and streaming down, flooding the roads and into the lakes. I made a call at Dove Cottage and saw it as Wordswoth must often have done, the cottage and the daffodils dripping. For memories' sake I bought a book from the shop by the cottage then set off for the rest of my journey. That day the rain was not confined to the Lakes for it continued the rest of the 300 miles, back to Essex and home.

From Langdale across Coniston to the sea.

The sky is high...
The mountains are high...
The clouds are high...
But sometimes clouds
Come down to the mountains...
And it makes rain
To keep the lakes full of Lake!

Aileen Otley.

Ullswater

An
Essex
Potpourri

THE CASTLE TIME FORGOT

THE BLACKMORE BUNCH

A MEDIEVAL MASTERPIECE

THE STUBBERS WALLED GARDEN

A FITTING MEMORIAL

A SNOWY VALENTINE

THE COLNE VALLEY RAILWAY

AN ESSEX PRINCESS

Some of the million primroses at the Primrose Festival, Bypass Nurseries, Marks Tey.

They call it –
"THE CASTLE TIME FORGOT"

When the Normans invaded England in 1066, they came ashore at Pevensey, close by one of the Roman Forts of The Saxon Shore; a fort built as part of a string around the south east coast to keep the Saxons at bay. Now the Saxons held sway in England under King Harold, who made a forced march from the north to resist William of Normandy. Their armies met: Harold and his men on Senlac Hill, William and his army on a hill about 400 yards away, on ground not quite as high as Senlac. Battle was joined and the slaughter continued all day. Harold was killed, his army defeated, and the Saxon simple way of life gave way to the more flamboyant style of the Normans : the course of our history changed forever.

Top: Pevensey, Roman 'Anderidos' a 4th Century fort of the Saxon Shore with Norman 12th century castle within.

Left: Battle, site of the Battle of Hastings. The battle field is beyond the abbey (top right)

William the Conqueror, as the new King came to be called, was very astute; he turned out most of the Saxon landholders of Essex at the conquest. Some of the land he kept; the remainder he distributed, in return for military and other services, to the army of fortune-seeking adventurers who came over with him. The County of Essex had about ninety landlords, and to aid the defence of their lands, castles were built, mostly of the Motte and Bailey type. Although the buildings of these castles have long since gone, throughout the county the classic shape of the Motte (an earth mound) and the Bailey (an outer enclosed area) castle can still be seen, notably, Rayleigh, Ongar, Pleshey and of course Stansted.

The site at Stansted is believed to have been first, an Iron Age Fort, (from about 700BC. to mid first century AD.) then to have been Viking and Saxon settlements. Standing now as it does close by the great airport bearing the same name, the Norman castle, Stansted Mountfitchet, has been reconstructed.

In 1066 the Saxon site was attacked by the Normans under Robert Gernon, the Duke of Boulougne and he made Stansted the chief seat of his barony. The Gernon family continued there for five generations, then William his son and heir dropped the name Gernon and adopted Montfitchet, a name which has been subsequently used by his descendants, and is the name by which the castle

Above: Pleshey Motte and Bailey Castle frost covered in January. Below: Stansted Mountfitchet

is known today. Some of the history is a little clouded, but it is known that Richard de Montfitchet joined the Baronial opposition to the King which resulted in the Magna Carta at Runnymede in 1215. At the time, and in spite of his youth, (he was 25) Richard was one of twenty-five barons chosen to enforce the observance of Magna Carta. Henry Laver in his article, 'The Castle of Stansted Mountfitchet', describes Richard de Montfitchet as "the youngest, yet one of the three bravest Knights in England."

church decorated with wall paintings designed to tell the gospel story to the illiterate occupants of the castle, for the priest was likely to be the only literate member of the Castle community.

Within the inner bailey is the Grand Hall, the central focus of the Castle. Here the Baron entertained his guests, held meetings and conducted trials.

Displayed on the wall of the Grand Hall are the shields of the 25 Barons who forced King John to sign and observe the Magna Carta.

Stansted Airport

Richard died without heir in 1258, the estate was divided between his three sisters and so came the end of the reign of the Montfitchets.

Stones were taken from the castle by the villagers to build their houses and the Castle site lay desolate, overgrown and forgotten for 700 years: that is, until today. Now, on this ancient site, the castle has been reborn.

Stansted Mountfichet is protected by the Department of the Environment and they only gave permission for the reconstruction providing none of the timeworn earth was disturbed. The result is a marvellous reconstruction which is freestanding, although the observer is unaware of the fact. An army of specialist craftsmen were put to work and the result is a Motte-and-Bailey castle with its Norman buildings, still with some Saxon and Viking influences showing today, just as they were in the 12th century.

You can enter through the main gate, decorated with severed heads, a warning to likely wrongdoers. Within the bailey, animals and birds wander free, much as they would have done in those far off days. Entering the buildings, sounds of the past and a description of the activities comes on. You can see most of the crafts of the times, the surgeon at work, (he was also the barber), the

One of the shields is that of Richard de Montfitchet.

A visit is a unique experience, bringing to life the atmosphere of 12th century Norman England.

The Grand Hall, Stansted Mountfitchet

The Blackmore Bunch

When the Romans fled this country in the mid 5th century they left us a legacy of fine buildings and a network of superb roads. The Romans were replaced by the much simpler East Saxons who settled down in isolated communities and homesteads. The Saxons had little time for the straight, well-planned and well-built roads they had inherited. Instead they wandered from cottage to inn, from inn to farm, from farm to church and market. Slowly, the Roman roads went into decay: they became overgrown and forgotten while gradually a new pattern of 'ways' was built up; in rural Essex the crooked footpaths, bridleways and byroads wound their devious routes, confounding many a traveller, but still lending charm to the countryside today.

Mountnessing, The Roman Road, (The Great Essex Road); Mountnessing Post Mill (c1807) and 'The Prince of Wales'

Little changed through the middle ages: then, in 1555, came the Highways Act, when each parish had to elect two surveyors and householders to work and repair the roads on four appointed days each year. Some improvement occurred and the old Roman roads had come back into use. In early March 1590 The Great Essex Road was firm enough to carry Dorothy Wadham in Lady Petre's coach from Ingatestone to London. That road was the main route from Aldgate in London, an important Roman port, through Stratford, Romford, Brentwood and Chelmsford and so on to Colchester, (Roman Camulodunum) a main garrison. In fact the road changed little from the Roman period until the towns and villages were bypassed in very recent times. As a child I was often taken on holiday to a farm near Terling: then as we drove through Mountnessing, I often gazed at the windmill, standing derelict to the north of the road.

It is a post mill, standing there and dominating the surrounding countryside since 1807, a date painted on the crowntree (the main beam which supports the mill and on which it can be rotated into wind) but there had been windmills on the site for many years before that. Opposite the windmill is a pub, The Prince of Wales. The pub has been there even longer than the mill and perhaps occupies the site of an inn where the Roman soldiers took their refreshment on their long march to Cumulodunum. During the years the windmill turned and ground corn, the landlord from the Prince of Wales would 'pop across the road' and purchase some fresh ground flour to bake bread for the travellers.

To gain finance for the upkeep of roads, an act of Parliament was passed which allowed the erection of turnpike gates, and, in 1696, the first gate in Essex was set up at Mountnessing; between the pub and the windmill.

Recently the original cast iron plaque displaying the 'turnpike charges' was excavated; and this interesting 'document' can be read above the bar in the Prince of Wales.

Above: Mountnessing Post Mill. ***Below:*** *The Prince of Wales and the Tollgate Plaque.*

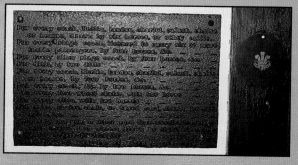

Between 1810 and 1937 Mountnessing Mill was owned and worked by four generations of the Agnis family, that is, until a sail was lost and the mill became derelict. Then in 1975, 'Friends of Mountnessing Mill' was formed and together with Essex County Council who appointed Mr. Vincent Pargeter as Millwright in the Planning Department, plans were made to restore the mill to working condition.

Work progressed, and in September 1979 three Blackmore girls saw the fundraising appeal and decided to help. Calling themselves 'The Blackmore Bunch', Wendy Schweitzer 8, Paula Sargeant ,11 and Sally Caplin decided to help. The three youngsters did a sponsored cycle ride round the village, set up a model windmill on Blackmore Village Green and handed over the money, mostly pennies, to the 'Friends' on the mill open day.

On the 13th of November 1983, the restored, early nineteenth century mill was opened, and a few days later a token amount of flour was produced again, for the first time in almost 50 years.

Now the sails can be seen turning again. Each month, flour is once again ground and can be purchased, although not in quantities enough to supply the Prince of Wales, where they still bake bread for their patrons.

I expect when the members of the 'Blackmore Bunch' pass the mill and see the giant sails slowly turning, they have a tinge of pride when they remember the pennies they raised to help it happen.

The Blackmore Bunch in 1979. Wendy Schweitzer, Paula Sargeant and Sally Caplin. Inset: Paula Threadgold, nee Sargeant, June 1993.

A Medieval Masterpiece

Great Canfield with Motte and Bailey Castle.

GREAT CANFIELD

Set on a tiny by-road close to the Roman road from Ongar to Great Dunmow is the beautiful village of Great Canfield. Behind the church and cottages, trees cover a mound which rises 50 feet above the village: beyond are the outer defences of the Norman motte-and-bailey castle. Both the mound and bailey are surrounded by a moat; now dry, but in ancient times filled by waters from the nearby River Roding. This tree-clad relic was once the mighty castle home of Aubrey de Vere, Great Chamberlain of England 800 years ago. It is likely that the castle was built of timber, of which nothing remains. But the little church, close by the moat, where Aubrey de Vere worshipped, has lost nothing of its ancient charm, and is a most perfect example of a Norman building. The walls stand as the Normans built them: only the bell turret which was added later postdates the original building. The doorways are richly carved, the mason chose hard stone and much of the delicate detail still survives.

Left: *The church of St. Mary.*
Inset: *Norman carving on doorway*

A MEDIEVAL MASTERPIECE

Inside the church the chancel arch is designed to form a perfect frame for the group of arches over the altar. There, set in a niche above the altar is a wall painting which is both a rare and beautiful masterpiece, as old as any in the National Gallery and the work of an English artist. The Madonna clothed in a yellow robe is nursing the Infant Jesus; Mary sits tranquil on a throne, raised on a dais. Experts think she was sitting serenely above the altar when Robert de Vere set out from the nearby castle for Runnymede and the signing of Magna Carta.

Luck played part in the survival of the painting, Sir William Wyseman and his family became powerful in Great Canfield and an elaborate monument showing Sir William holding the hand of his wife was placed in front of the altar so they could use the niche as a background. It was only in recent times when the monument was removed that the wall painting was revealed for us all to wonder at and enjoy.

Church of St. Mary, Great Canfield.

The Madonna and Child (13th Century).

The Stubbers Walled Garden.

Stubbers Walled Garden. Note the Crinkle-Crankle Wall.

About a mile from the the beautiful and ancient church at North Ockendon was a large house of the 16th century, complete with its early barn and a large fish pond. The pond was to supply the household with fresh fish, usually carp, and very often a kitchen garden would be built to supply the house with fruit and vegetables. Nothing remains of this manor house, save the name, Manor Farm, which is near the site, and Stubbers Walled Garden a short distance away. Usually, as at Stubbers the garden would be 'walled.'

WALLED GARDENS

Walled gardens date back to the middle ages and especially the monasteries, where the monks endeavoured to make their community self sufficient. Tall walls, usually created in a rectangular form, moderated the wind, trapped the sun and produced a gentle, almost tropical climate within. The vast areas of walls were used to support fruit trees and other climbing plants; and sometimes a 'crin-kle-crankle' wall was built to give both increased strength and a greater area of use. Very often beside our native apple, pear and plum, fig, peach and other exotic fruit and plants could be seen growing within the favourable environment created by the walls.

WILLIAM COYS

William Coys lived at Stubbers between 1580 and 1627 and while there he built five, possibly six, walled gardens; of which, the garden at Stubbers is the most noteworthy. He obtained over 324 varieties of plants, many from abroad which were growing at Stubbers for the very first time in this country.

It was only about one hundred years since Columbus discovered America and already explorers were sailing to the many new lands. The crews returned not only with strange tales and treasure, but also exotic plants and seeds the likes of which had not been seen here before. It is surprising that at such an early date so much interest should have been shown in the plants, shrubs and trees the explorers brought home.

William Coys garden was formally arranged, which was typical of the period, especially when the garden was placed near the house it served, so that the designs could be admired from the upper windows. However, at Stubbers the garden was created away from the house so as not to obstruct views of the landscaped gardens around the building and the superb avenue of lime trees called 'The Lime Tree Walk'. It is difficult to imagine now that the many plants we take for granted, for instance the tomato, rhubarb, peonies and pansies, were growing there and had never before been seen in England. L'Obel, after whom Lobelia is named, visited Coys in 1604 and saw *Yucca Gloriosa* flowering at Stubbers for the first time.

Coys mantained contact with many eminent botanists of his day and much of what is known about the content of Stubbers comes from lists made by John Goodyer. John visited the gardens in 1617, 1621, and 1622, when he made lists, in latin, of the plants he observed there. These lists are probably the earliest manuscripts of the contents of an English garden, albeit many of the plants originating from far away. John Goodyer saw the Ivy Leaved Toadflax growing on the walls at Stubbers; now this pretty plant is widespread thoughout the country, and still graces the walled garden just as it did in William Coy's day.

THE FRIENDS OF STUBBERS WALLED GARDEN.

Alas the house and the landscaped garden have long since gone; the Lime Tree Avenue survived until the middle of this century, however the Walled Garden, much derelict, and the crinkle-crankle wall survived, and have now been much restored. Now the aim of the 'Friends of Stubbers Walled Garden' is to reconstruct the interior of the garden in the manner and style of the early seventeenth century. And it is planned to incorporate as many of the plants named by L'Obel and listed by John Goodyer, and wherever possible the original Elizabethan types will be planted.

When complete, Stubbers Walled Garden will provide a fascinating peep into one part of the life of an English manor house.

Louise Sinclair, Mayor of Havering, visits Stubbers Walled Garden.

Inset: July 1993, tending the garden.

'A Fitting Memorial'
To a Very Funny Man!

When I take people flying either for a flying lesson or perhaps, on an airborne sightseeing tour of Essex, as you might expect, I often find myself at one of my favourite places, the River Blackwater where its broad expanse stretches from Maldon to the sea. While there is a small dispute about the source of the river, its life certainly begins where it springs from the ground not too far from Saffron Walden, deep in the Essex countryside. There the river starts a slow meander through lush fields, past villages whose history extends back into the distant past. In fact, one possible place where the river rises is close by Tiptofts an early 14th century house. Here, in a field, a change of colour indicates the presence of water: then the trickle becomes a tiny stream as it mingles with a spring close by the moat which still surrounds the house. Many of the ancient houses, in which Essex is rich, have undergone changes through the centuries; but here at Tiptofts is a superb example of a manor house where the touch of time has been minimal. The main hall has survived virtually unchanged since about the time when the Plantagenet King, Edward I, created the first Prince of Wales. The river here is known as the Pant, a name it keeps for about half its journey to Maldon: then, as it flows past Bocking, it becomes The River Blackwater, but its character changes little until it reaches Maldon where it joins with the Chelmer and spreads out into a broad expanse of water, so wide, that there is some thought that this was once part of a mighty Thames Estuary.

River Pant flows under Bocking and emerges as the River Blackwater.

The River Blackwater. Inset: Waders in flight over the Blackwater. Photo: Gerry Downy

Each side of this magnificent river has fortunately escaped the worst of man's ravages. Some of the villages now sport a marina but these do not detract too much from the charm of the riverside. The only blot on this beautiful seascape is the vast nuclear power station at Bradwell.

With its wide expanses of shallow water, saltings and marshes the estuary has been a haven for thousands of birds for countless years. Waders, ducks and gulls make it their home, and during the winter thousands of migrating wildfowl come to overwinter and feed in the gentler climes of Essex. In days gone by many thousands of ducks were trapped in decoy ponds, of which about thirty were along each bank of the Blackwater: then the ducks were dispatched to the markets of London. Now apart from some shooting, the river and marshes has increasing numbers of bird-lovers who visit the remote regions. Here they enjoy the great natural spectacle provided by the large variety and vast number of birds in the estuary.

Between the western end of Mersea Island and the village of Tollesbury lies a peninsula, which is almost an island. This desolate tract of marshland, complete with the remnants of a medieval decoy pond, is known as Old Hall Marshes. I suppose there was an Old Hall nearby at one time, now all one can see from the air is the wilderness home of thousands of birds.

Some years ago this wonderful place came up for sale. Eric Morecambe, one of the countries best loved comedians, and himself a member of the RSPB and a great bird lover, died.

So the RSPB set up the Eric Morecambe Memorial Appeal, and as part of that appeal on the 1st November 1985 a Royal Gala Concert in the presence of Her Royal Highness Princess Alexandra, was presented at the Barbican. The concert was wonderful and a great success; it included, pointedly, Handel's Water Music Suite and concluded with Beethoven's Pastoral (no 6) Symphony. In this, Beethoven expressed in music, inspired by a landscape at a riverside, of birdcalls, of storms and shepherds, his own feelings for the countryside he loved so much.

The money raised at that concert, and from the appeal went to purchase Old Hall Harshes. After a lifetime of giving pleasure to millions, Eric Morecambe's memorial gives haven to millions of birds which grace our fields with their colour and their plaintive calls: thousands sweep down onto the marshes out of the winter sky.

Now when I fly above Old Hall Marshes I turn the aircraft slowly around the area and tell my passengers about Eric and his concert: then they almost always remark, "What a fitting memorial to a very funny man!"

Old Hall Marshes. **Inset:** *The late Eric Morecambe*

A Snowy Valentine.

For some years snow and winter had not seriously come together in Essex. Then, towards mid February 1991, the snows came; not much, but enough to produce a white winter mantle over the countryside. For a long time I had wanted some pictures of Essex snow covered; and particularly the area around Hadleigh and Two Tree Island, near Southend. February the 12th brought the snow with heavy falls in the late afternoon and evening. The next day the snow had stopped falling and when I went to Southend Airport, the sun was shining fitfully, enough to make the pictures interesting but, fortunately not with sufficient strength to melt the snow. Ice and frost covered the aircraft, aeroplanes become different like that. It is not just the extra weight: in particular, the covering of ice on the wings and control surfaces change the aircraft's performance; making it very difficult or impossible to take off. So before flying it had to be de-iced. One hour later, after a lot of de-icing fluid had been sprayed on the 'Cessna 152', the residue scrapped off and our energy expended, the aircraft was clear and we were ready to go. Alan Ward, another pilot, was to fly the aircraft while I was to take the pictures. After take off on runway 24 (

that is 240° from north, to the southwest) we turned left and headed south towards the coast. Two Tree Island had its several thousand over-wintering Brent Geese; to them it must have looked more like their Siberian home. Snow covered Leigh on Sea sparkled in the faint winter sunlight, while perched on its knoll a little to the west, looking even more desolate than usual, stood Hadleigh Castle.

As always when enjoying a flight, the minutes ticked away all to quickly and it was time to turn for home. Then, quite by chance I looked down at Hadleigh, and there quite clearly, within a vast rectangle was the 'valentine' 'I LOVE RUTH' 'carved' in the snow. The message had, in view of its medium, a very transient life; although the content could be everlasting. Out came the camera, and while the little aircraft circled John Burrow's recreation ground, I ensured that the message would have a longer life than the snow.

Intrigued, and having a romantic nature, I took the film to the Evening Echo where the editor said he would like to print it and ask for our latter day Romeo and Juliet to make themselves known. The next day, St. Valentine's day, the declaration was there for all to see, for 'I

Soon we had the answer: the Sweethearts were Ruth Raphael and Nathan Haisman-Baker. She said:

"It was our six-month anniversary of going together and also Nathan's birthday. We had been for a drink in a nearby pub and as we were walking back across the cricket field when Nathan saw this patch of untrodden snow. He just stopped and jumped over the fence then shuffled the message out with his feet."

The romantic gesture might never have been, for the very snow which made the 'Valentine' possible was coming down in a blizzard as Nathan made his way to Ruth for his birthday celebration. However, the fall had stopped by the time they had left the pub and Nathan created his Valentine. Strangely, the gigantic message, perhaps the largest Valentine ever, could only be seen completely from an aircraft.

Ruth remarked to Nathan, "Wouldn't it be wonderful if we could have a photograph of that! Never knowing that the next day the Evening Echo's 'Spy in The Sky' would be in the air to record it. But that is how the long arm of romance works.

This is now mid June in 1993. I have spoken with Ruth today and she told me: "Nathan and I are still very much in love, we are engaged and are looking forward to being married in the near future."

Ruth Raphael and Nathan Haisman-Baker.

THE LEGEND OF ST. VALENTINE.

Legend has it that St. Valentine was in a prison cell and from the window
he picked some violets and sent them by a dove:

And on the violets' velvet leaves
He pierced these lines divine
That simply said, "I LOVE YOU"
And I'M YOUR VALENTINE"...
So through the years that followed,
From that day to this,
Folks still send messages of love
And seal them with a kiss...

Helen Steiner Rice

The Colne Valley Railway.

As I move about the country I continue to be amazed at the number of individuals and societies set up to preserve varied fragments of our interesting and colourful past. We have read of the Friends of Stubbers Walled Garden in the south; in the north, amongst others, there is The Stour Valley Railway Preservation Society. The society was set up in September 1968 with the object of reopening the whole or part of The Stour Valley Railway.

Chappel Viaduct and the museum

Chappel and Wakes Colne Station

British Rail were in the process of closing many branch lines and already time was all important. Demolition gangs were stripping out signal boxes, rails were being torn up, engine sheds left derelict. So it was at Chappel and Wakes Colne Station when, on the 4th December 1970, The Stour Valley Railway Preservation Society obtained a lease from British Rail. Chappel Station is on the northern side of the marvellous viaduct built by the Victorians to carry their railway across the River Colne. This viaduct is the largest still in use in the eastern counties and its seven million bricks built into 12 arches is an elegant reminder of the railway builders skills.

At Chappel the track, already dismantled, was in a shed awaiting the scrap merchant; it was saved, members set to work and within 100 days the society was able to have a 'steam day' and passengers were once again able to enjoy the distinctive smells and sounds of a steam locomotive, albeit only on a third of a mile of track. Now the signal box and the engine sheds together with several sections of line have been restored, and although only operating over a very limited distance, on 'steam days' the 'railway' is run with the precision and discipline of a 'full grown' system.

The signal box is open and in there you can talk to the society president and signal man, Mr B.D.J.Walsh. From there the engine already steaming can be seen as it waits

Society President and Signalman, Mr. B.D.J. Walsh.

ready to pull a 'proper corridor train'. The passengers have boarded and the guard is awaiting the signal. The signalman (Mr Walsh) sets the 'starter signal', the guard blows his whistle and checks all the doors are closed, then he gives the driver 'the green flag'. The engine whistle sounds and the train moves slowly out of the station, and as the train passes the signal box, because it is entering a single line track the fireman is passed a token. Only one token exists, so the fireman knows there is no other train on the track, and it is safe to proceed. The token is then handed back to the signalman on the train's return when it vacates the single track line.

Since his boyhood, Mr. Walsh wanted to be a railwayman, especially, of course, a driver but that was not to be. Unfortunately he wore glasses and in those days that was not accepted on the railways. Now, after a professional life as a lawyer, he is able to indulge his lifelong passion at Chappel.

CASTLE HEDINGHAM

From Chappel, the 'main line', which is still operated by British Rail, using its own track through Chappel and Wakes Colne station, follows the valley of the River Stour through Long Melford then turns west continuing to follow the River Stour to Shelford, another branch goes to Bury St. Edmonds.

At Chappel also, the track divides and what was the Colne Valley & Halstead Railway ran north west along the valley of the River Colne through Halstead to Haverhill. Passing as it does through some of the loveliest Essex countryside, the train journey must have been a delight. Along the route is Castle Hedingham, and as its name implies it is the site of a great Norman Castle: its keep, one of the finest in the country, stands high and dominates the area.

Here, re-created in green fields, is a sample of an East Anglian Country Railway. Relocated station buildings, bridges and signal boxes have all been lovingly restored and now house a collection of operational vintage engines and carriages.

Both Chappel and Castle Hedingham are not just museums, wonderful though museums are, but are 'working railways' where volunteer workers strive to restore locomotives, rolling stock and all the associated equipment to their past glory. Then on 'Steam Days' operate the system for our pleasure. A visit to either will transport you back in time, so that you can sample once again the sights, smells and sounds from the 'Golden Age Of Steam.'

Left: Castle Hedingham Railway Museum.

Below: Passing the token.

Bottom: Recreating the 'Golden Age Of Steam' at Chappel and Wakes Colne Station.

An Essex Princess

The River Roding, before it finishes its journey ingloriously at Barking Creek where it enters the Thames, meanders through miles of Essex countryside, giving grace to many a small village. At Fyfield the main street and the willow-shaded River Roding wind side by side through the village and, close by the river stands the church, dedicated to St. Nicholas and built by the Normans in a grand way during the 12th century. By that time the art of brick and tile making, introduced by the Romans, who finding little stone in Essex, used the fine clay to fashion superb brick and tile, had been forgotten. So, within the heritage of fine buildings abandoned by the Romans some 600 years earlier,

ble hypocaust (an underfloor central heating system) of a Roman villa were discovered. It seems likely that it was from this villa that the material in Fyfield church came. A couple of miles further south the gentle river winds its path through High Ongar.

Behind the Red Lion pub, and close by the river is a small group of allotments: it was here that the 'Princess' came to life. Sam Shuttleworth has cultivated one of these patches for many years, but as well as providing vegetables for the dinner table, Sam has indulged his passion for growing roses which has produced prize blooms and won awards at Rose Shows all round the country. Not content with producing winners from exist-

Fyfield. Church of St. Nicholas. Inset: Excavation of Roman Villa at Ongar.

medieval builders found a ready made 'quarry' and used the material from the Roman buildings, especially in the churches. Here, at Fyfield Roman tiles can be seen in the nave, and through an opening in the tower the Norman masons shaped the Roman tile into the round newel of the staircase.

The River Roding wends its way south past a farm where only last year (1992) the foundations, and possi-

ing varieties, Sam's ambition was to create a variety of his own. Much thought, crossbreeding and cultivating went on for many years: then at last he was satisfied. A floribunda rose of delicate yellow colour and with the distinctive rose smell bloomed for the first time on the little patch of ground; and Sam decided to call it "Fyfield Princess".

Fyfield

On the 5th January 1992, the Chairman of Ongar Council planted a group of the new roses in a little garden by the side of St Nicholas Church, close by the River Roding. Now if you visit Fyfield in the summer, there beside the church you can meet the 'Fyfield Princess'.

Morning a thousand Roses brings, you say;
Yes, but where leaves the Rose of yesterday?
And this first Summer month that brings the Rose
Shall take Jamshyd and Kaikobád away.

Omar Khayyám.